César

To [?] Doug from the Olivieman

César

RECIPES FROM A TAPAS BAR

Olivieman   *James Mellgren*

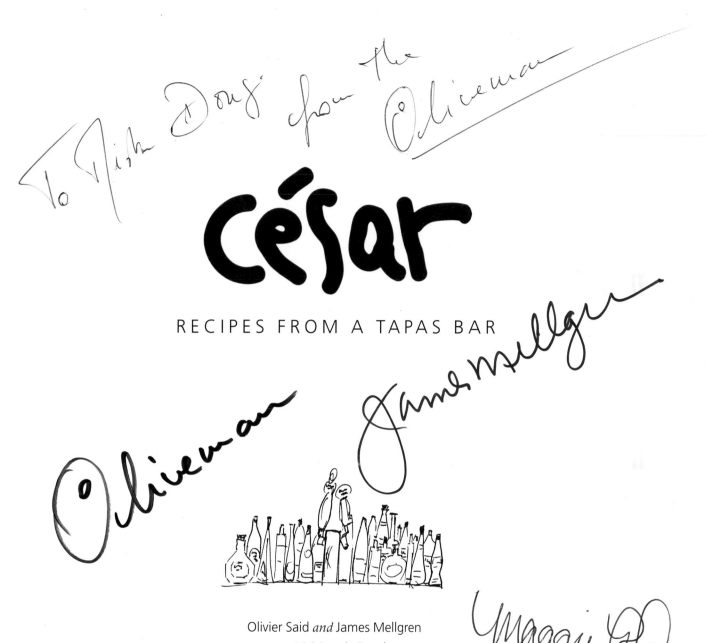

Olivier Said *and* James Mellgren
with Maggie Pond

Maggie Po

Foreword *by* Jackson Browne

Ten Speed Press
Berkeley / Toronto

Ten Speed Press
Box 7123
Berkeley, California 94707
www.tenspeed.com

Distributed in Australia by Simon & Schuster Australia, in Canada by Ten Speed Press Canada, in New Zealand by Southern Publishers Group, in South Africa by Real Books, and in the United Kingdom and Europe by Airlift Book Company.

Book design by James Wilson

Library of Congress Cataloging-in-Publication Data
Said, Olivier.
  César: recipes from a tapas bar / Olivier Said and James Mellgren with Maggie Pond ; photography by Olivier Said.
      p. cm.
  ISBN 1-58008-483-4
  1. Appetizers. 2. Cocktails. 3. Cookery, Spanish. I. Mellgren, James. II. Pond, Maggie. III. Title.
  TX740 .S22 2003
  641.8'12--dc21
                        2003009248

Printed in Hong Kong
First printing, 2003

1 2 3 4 5 6 7 8 9 10 — 07 06 05 04 03

To the families of restaurateurs everywhere.

Contents

Acknowledgments

The authors would like to begin their thanks with César's founders and owners, Richard Mazzera, Dennis Lapuyade, and Stephen Singer, the royal triumvirate who set the standard of professionalism, yet kept reminding us that the book should be fun.

To designer James Wilson, whose creativity helped shape the book and infuse it with color, both literally and metaphorically.

We would all like to send thanks to Megan Micco, whose spirit and creativity contributed mightily to this book.

Thanks go to bartender Kathleen Ventura, who has been there from the beginning, and whose skills are not limited to mixing drinks.

We also want to thank sous chef Mil Apostol and head cook Germain Andrade for maintaining high standards in the kitchen.

Special thanks to architect John Holey, who designed César; and to Collin Carrell, who helped build it.

We would like to thank recipe testers Annette Flores, Kappy Sugawara, and Anthony Sperber.

Very special thanks go to Joan Lapuyade, who not only tirelessly tested recipes and kept the books, but also entertained us and kept us going through it all.

Big thanks go to copyeditor Rebecca Pepper, proofreader Sharon Silva, and indexer Ken Della Penta for their work on the book.

Thanks to Dennis Hayes at Ten Speed Press for believing in the project and bringing us together. A special thanks to Ten Speed owner Phil Wood for loving restaurants so much, and to editorial director Lorena Jones for putting up with a bunch of neophytes. An enormous thanks goes to our editor, Aaron Wehner, who made it all seem so easy.

Maggie would like to give personal thanks to her parents, Katherine and Richard Pond, and her grandmother, Helen Edney, for teaching her how to enjoy food.

Maggie would also like to thank David Tanis, founding chef, for setting the standard that we strive to uphold every day.

James would like to thank his wife, Sydney, who tested recipes, kept the home fires burning, and for saying she likes his cocktails best.

The success of bar César has been due to the hard work and collaboration of a highly skilled team of bartenders, cooks, waiters, and bussers who toil nightly to keep the chaos looking like a well choreographed dance. To the entire staff of César, past and present, a big thank you.

And finally, a bar is only as good as the people who patronize it, and in that respect we are lucky indeed. A huge thanks to the people of Berkeley who have embraced César and who keep coming back. Again and again and again . . .

Foreword
by Jackson Browne

Every time I return from Spain, I set about trying to convert my California existence into something more like the time I've just spent eating and drinking with friends, and exploring the cultures and traditions of the country that has captured my attention and fueled my imagination for several years. It's not an easy thing to do, to turn one place into another.

I buy Spanish wines and cheeses, look for Spanish olive oil, wait for the infrequent flamenco touring companies, and try to find Spain in the smattering of Spanish restaurants in Los Angeles. And where are the Spanish restaurants?

I walk everywhere I go when I'm in Barcelona, so I try walking to and from work for a while, but in L. A. this only seems like a waste of time. Maybe if the whole city, no, the whole country, shut down everyday at noon or one o'clock, and kids came home from school, parents came home from work, the streets filled up with people walking to, and meeting in, restaurants, and everywhere people were taking the best part of the day to be with their friends, their families, or their lovers until around four or five o'clock when business resumed—then maybe California would be made into Spain. But it's more than lunch, more than the siesta, more than the enormous opening in the middle of the day through which an entire country passes. It's the way the Spanish measure their lives in terms of how well they enjoy themselves.

At the news that friends were planning to open a tapas bar in Berkeley, I felt the tug of a familiar longing, mixed with a little apprehension. Could they do it? Spain is not just Spain—it's the Mediterranean and the Atlantic, the Pyrenees and two borders with France. In Spanish food there is the inherent and underlying value of discovery and innovation, combined with tradition, fueled by passion. On reflection, I realized that if anyone could do it, these particular Berkeley crazies could. And the Bay Area, with its proximity to the sea and to wine country, and its longstanding connection to the natural-food movement and to innovative food-growing practices—not to mention being the home of Chez Panisse, the most seminal influence upon

California cuisine—would be a likely host to their enterprise. Really, the more I thought about it, what could be more Spanish?

But perhaps you don't want to exchange your California existence for one more Mediterranean, Spanish or otherwise. Maybe you only want to leaven this life with something heretofore unexpected. Well then, here is a map, a manual, or as they say in Berkeley, a manifesto. A trail of crumbs and vapors, tastes and sensations, to lead you on, and a room in which to resume the search. For Spain? For California? Or—as California was called in its infancy—for New Spain?

Introduction

"A topless bar?!"
"No, a tapas bar. It's Spanish."
"And so you think that makes it alright then?"

In spite of construction mishaps, El Niño, byzantine building codes, and the thinly veiled disappointment of passersby that "tapas" meant little plates of food rather than bare-breasted bartenders, César opened its doors in May 1998 on a stretch of Berkeley's Shattuck Avenue that is affectionately known as the Gourmet Ghetto. It instantly became a hit among bar and restaurant cognoscenti from Berkeley and throughout the San Francisco Bay Area.

The transformation of the little dry cleaner next door to Chez Panisse into a modern American interpretation of a tapas bar began in the rainy days of January of the same year, during what was to become the wettest winter in recent history, and would continue through the barely controlled chaos created by a team of self-styled carpenters who would make the Keystone Kops look like the Bolshoi Ballet. The owners of Chez Panisse had secured the lease on the space in order to have a say in what would open next door. A trio of Chez Panisse expatriates, having decided to go out on their own, signed a sublease and, convinced that there were no good bars in Berkeley, elected to build one. With their famous neighbor as an inspiration and standard bearer, they would use only the finest and freshest ingredients for their cocktails, adhering to classic recipes and intelligent, original creations, and would stock an ever-changing, eclectic list of wines, sherries, whiskeys, and brandies. And food. They wanted to serve bar food that would complement the cocktails, yet be good enough to be a draw in itself. If next door they served great wines to accompany their inspired food, then César would serve food to accompany their inspired drinks.

All agreed that they didn't want to imitate the food at Chez Panisse, except in the quality of the raw materials. If Chez Panisse was a culmination of French and Italian influences, then this bar would take a slight culinary detour on the Mediterranean road map and feature tapas, the little dishes of Spain. The name came from a charming thirties-era film trilogy about life in a sleepy quayside bar in Marseilles. The films by Marcel Pagnol—*Marius, Fanny,* and *César*—had already inspired the name of Alice Waters's restaurant thirty years before (Panisse is one of the central characters in the trilogy). The character of César, played by the great French actor Raimu, was the father to Marius and owner of the Bar de la Marine. Please note, if you ever see the films, that César is much busier than the bar in the films. Everyone there seems to spend their time talking, playing cards, and drinking pastis. Come to think of it, that's pretty much how César is run, only with a lot more customers.

There is an old Italian saying that it takes four people to make a proper salad dressing: a miser to pour the vinegar, a spendthrift for the oil, a wise man to add the salt, and a mad man to mix it all up. In hindsight, this is an apt metaphor for building a bar, especially when the owners opt to do it themselves in order to conserve resources. One of the owners, Richard Mazzera, foolishly assumed the role of general contractor, abetted by a merry band of constructioneers. Then, after hours of playing with expensive software, they had an epiphany and hired architect John Holey, who translated Richard's basic design into a workable and beautiful plan. Construction continued apace, analogous to a snowball that starts rolling down a long, steep hill.

On the following page is a list, based on the experience of opening César, for those of you out there who have similar fantasies about opening a bar or a restaurant—a list that should persuade you to immediately abandon all such ideas.

The César Construction Checklist

- First make a list.

- Be aware that the list of things to do never gets shorter; it only gets longer—sort of like a black hole of tasks.

- Get a tool kit. It should consist of Velcro, duct tape, a jackhammer, and Band-Aids.

- Get a first aid kit. It should consist of Velcro, duct tape, and 151-proof rum.

- Nail pullers are always more important than nail pounders.

- Choose your help by how many tools they own. Whoever owns a pick-up truck is the head carpenter.

- Procure a beautiful Douglas fir dining room table that can seat more than twelve people and can also be used to hold a table saw or a drill press. (This table was a silent witness to the realization of César and now sits proudly in the middle of the bar.)

- Install the stereo system. Not only is it good for the morale of the workers, but it will give you at least one desperately needed sense of accomplishment.

- Wait until the first heavy rains begin, and then tear off the roof.

- Never point with the hand that is operating the circular saw.

- Never change the blade while the saw is running. At the very least, it is extremely hot.

- At lunchtime, clear the workbench–communal table, and set out candles, food, and wine. (Wine merchant–friend Kermit Lynch provided support throughout in the form of magnum bottles of Châteauneuf-du-Pape and Bandol rosé.)

- When tiling a wall, after the mortar has dried, claim that it was exactly the design you wanted.

- You will know when to stop tiling when one of the following occurs: you run out of tiles or you run out of wine.

- Wait until you have closed up the walls, and then call the plumbing and electrical inspectors.

- The most productive meetings happen when you're alone.

- Group decisions are best made based not on who's there, but on who's not there.

- Option One: When construction is complete, clean up and open the bar.

- Option Two: When the money runs out, stop construction, clean up, and open the bar.

- On the first day, open the doors when the bread arrives or the paint dries, whichever comes first.

Opening the Doors

In the end, patience, perseverance, and a good Shop-Vac prevailed, and César opened its doors to the awaiting and thirsty public. It was immediately clear that tapas were the ideal food complement for the bar, as evidenced by the enthusiastic response from the locals, as well as the newspaper reviews that followed. A curious thing happened after our three-star review appeared in one of the San Francisco dailies, a review in which we were admonished for the inadequate size of our paper napkins. New customers began showing up with their own napkins, apparently afraid they would be left dripping at the bar with nothing to clean themselves but their sleeves. People who had actually been to tapas bars in Spain had a laugh because our napkins are considerably larger than the tiny, coarse, square serviettes issued abroad. In an act of defiance that our detractors would say is the equivalent of a schoolyard "am not, are too" debate, we have refused to change the size of our napkins, and patrons are free to use as many as they want.

With or without napkins, the tapas menu has been a hit, and it continues to intrigue the staff and delight the customers. The decision to offer tapas also brought a commitment to seeking out the best traditional Spanish ingredients, and to annual sojourns to Spain by chef Maggie Pond to eat, learn, cook, and generally soak up Spanish life and food. This has not been a particularly odious task for Maggie, who has fallen in love with Spain, as most visitors eventually do. Every time Maggie returns from the Iberian Peninsula, she arrives armed with new ideas, new recipes, and an expanded knowledge of ingredients.

Absinthe Makes the Heart Grow Fonder

Since it opened in the spring of 1998, César has become known as a hub of sophisticated nightlife in Berkeley: a place to see and be seen and, well, a darn good watering hole. In addition to the variety of tapas, Bay Area denizens have come to appreciate what many agree are the finest cocktails in town (including San Francisco, across the bridge) and an endlessly fascinating selection of wines and spirits. The collection of sherries alone would make César a worthy destination, especially for those with a predilection for all things Spanish. César combines the best of authentic contemporary Spanish tapas with the uniquely American art of the cocktail.

We have tried to capture some of the spirit of César in these pages—the lively and irreverent atmosphere, the elegant design, and the various victuals and libations for which the bar is known. We are sure that Olivier's photographs will help bring the place to life for you, revealing a bit of both the backstage happenings and the front-of-the-house melee that occurs nightly. We will also impart some serious information about the myriad artisanal food products from Spain, bartending tips and lore gleaned from years behind the bar, and, of course, recipes for tapas and cocktails for your own entertaining and entertainment.

In documenting the chaotic life that is the restaurant business, the partners have had time to reflect on the combined years of experience that have led to César. Dennis Lapuyade's thirty-five years in the business are added to the more than two generations that his family has run an auberge in the French Pyrenees. Olivier has been plying his craft for twenty-seven years, and his family has had restaurants in France since 1840. Richard Mazzera and Stephen Singer can each count more than twenty years as well. So you see this lunacy, this divine madness is in our collective blood. It is what we do and what we love. As Shakespeare said, "We few, we happy few, we band of brothers." Okay, so he was talking about going into battle, but then it could be said that running a restaurant each night is a cross between opening night on Broadway and laying siege to the citadel, so the analogy isn't far off.

Ultimately, this is a book about eating and drinking and having a good time. It's about a world-class bar, its secrets, its recipes, and the denizens who fill the seats each night and keep coming back in spite of the fact that our bartenders keep their shirts on.

César Index

Number of months it took to transform César from dingy dry cleaner to modern tapas bar:
4.5.

Number of tiles that were individually applied by three people:
78,000.

Number of tiles still on the walls:
77,987.

Number of loaves of Acme bread used since opening day:
29,200.

Number of Mojitos made:
23,000.

Number of orders of fried potatoes made:
50,000, or $235,000 worth.

Number of days in 2001 when no bar regular stopped in:
0.

Number of days in 2001 that César closed due to California's power shortages:
4.

Number of spirits and wines on hand at all times:
more than 450 of each, or 900 total.

Number of Margaritas made:
13,000.

Number of "last calls" announced to date:
1,790.

Number of broken glasses, not counting the construction phase:
5,000.

Number of times the alarm went off in the middle of the night for no reason:
  First two years: a lot.
  Third year: much less.
  Fourth year: almost none.
  Fifth year: not yet.

Number of espresso spoons lost:
10 dozen are ordered every 10 days.
(We know who you are, so bring them back.)

Glasses of wine consumed:
  By paying customers:174,000.
  Unaccounted for: divide by 10.
  By employees for quality control: divide by 5.

Number of Martinis made:
47,800.

Number of martini olives used:
70,000.

Number of customers who have come to César and not had a good time:
3.5.

Sherry

A night out in Spain usually begins with sherry, Spain's most famous libation, and although drinking habits are slowly changing there (as they are throughout the rest of Europe), sherry is still the most popular way to start the evening's procession through the tapas bars. American drinkers might argue in favor of the Martini or Manhattan as the preferred way to launch the night's festivities, but more and more consumers agree that sherry is the ultimate aperitif, especially the finos and manzanillas—light, refreshing quaffs that are worthy companions to a host of tapas. This is no surprise since it was in the roadside taverns throughout sherry-making country that the very idea of tapas was born.

Despite the cult status of sherry in Spain and its growing popularity in the United States, a great deal of confusion remains about its singular method of production and the wide range of styles in which sherry is made. As a fortified wine, sherry belongs, like port, both in the realm of wine and that of spirits, and yet it complements food in a way that most spirits or port can never do. The styles of sherry range from bone-dry finos and manzanillas to the seductively sweet creams and Pedro Ximénez varieties. In between lie the complex amontillados and olorosos, which in themselves can sway from dry to sweet, depending on the desires of the winemaker or, perhaps more importantly, on the desire of the wine itself.

Sherry typifies what French wine producers refer to as *terroir,* or the distinct qualitative influence of the soil, the climate, the geography, and other unique conditions on the wine. In the case of sherry, however, it has as much to do with the unique method of aging known as the solera system and the indigenous yeast-filled air currents that flow through the vaulted, white-washed attics of the sherry bodegas, as it does with the dazzlingly white *albariza* soil.

Sherry comes from a relatively small area in the southwest corner of Spain, in the region of Andalusia. Known as el Marco de Jerez, or the Sherry Triangle, it comprises Jerez de la Frontera (so named because it once sat on the frontier between the Catholic regions of the north and the Moorish-controlled south), Sanlúcar de Barrameda, and El Puerto de Santa María. The triangle is bound by two great rivers, the Guadalquivir and Guadalete, and by the Atlantic Ocean. This is the Spain of Carmen and bullfights, of equestrians and sun-baked, whitewashed villages. It is also the birthplace of tapas. The name itself has evolved through the centuries, in a succession of spellings from the Greeks, Romans, and Moors, to the current Castilian word, Jerez (pronounced hair-ETH), and the French equivalent, Xérès, that has been corrupted into the English vernacular as sherry. All three forms appear on labels, written as Jerez-Xérès-Sherry.

Sherry's history is tied as much to the sea as it is to the land. After all, it was down the Guadalquivir River from Seville that Columbus began his journey to the Americas, no doubt with plenty of sherry aboard for the crew. Early seafarers had learned that wine fortified with grape spirits would keep better on long voyages, and after Sir Francis Drake raided the port of Cádiz and plundered several hundred butts of sherry destined for the Spanish Armada, sherry became well known in England, thus starting sherry's international trade (the United Kingdom is still the largest importer of sherry).

The noble palomino grape makes up 95 percent of sherry production, with Pedro Ximénez (PX) and moscatel blended into some sherries for sweetness. The latter two grapes are cultivated in ever-decreasing quantities, and it is the palomino that reigns supreme in Jerez. Oddly, this grape makes a very ordinary white wine (although some young winemakers are trying to change that), low in both sugars and acid. It is, however, perfectly suited to the unique process that it will undergo. First, the grapes are crushed and lightly fermented in either glass or stainless-steel tanks, and then the wine is fortified with neutral grape spirits (basically brandy that has not been aged) to about 16 percent alcohol. After this initial fermentation, the wine is moved to large oak casks, and it is here that it takes a radical turn away from conventional winemaking techniques.

Normally, air and wine are natural enemies or, at best, surly bedfellows, but in the case of sherry they work in tandem, with the wine protected in part by the higher level of alcohol. The barrels are filled only about two-thirds full, allowing for a layer of air in the upper part. Soon a thin layer of natural yeast known as *flor* forms on the surface in some of the barrels. Not least among sherry's singular qualities is the ability of the wine to effectively decide its own fate. A barrel that develops a thick, healthy *flor* will become a dry, fino-style sherry, while one with little or no *flor* will turn into a sweeter, oloroso-style sherry. No one really understands why the *flor* grows in some barrels and not others, nor why, when the *flor* is taken out of the Jerez region, it withers and dies. In recent years, technology has flexed its muscles in Jerez, as it has done in the rest of the winemaking world, allowing sherry makers to have some control over the active yeasts. Nevertheless, this unique phenomenon is still a wonderful mystery, one that continues to add a bit of romance to the region and its wine.

Sherry spends the first year of its life in the damp ground floor of the bodega, with the gentle sea breezes performing their magic as the wine decides what it wants to be when it grows up. From here it goes through the most unusual aging method in the wine world. Rows of American oak barrels, or butts, are stacked in pyramids, three to five barrels high, in the cavernous attics of the bodegas. The bottom row is called the solera (from *suelo,* or "floor"), and it is from these butts that sherry to be bottled will be taken, although they are never emptied. After some of the sherry has been drawn off, an equal quantity is added from the row directly above, which in turn is replaced from the row above that, with the topmost row replenished with new wine in a cycle that has been repeated for generations. The mixing of old and new sherry creates the ultimate character of the wine or, as the sherry makers say, the older sherry gives character to the young wine, while the young wine gives vitality to the old. The following is a look at the various styles of sherries.

Manzanilla and Fino

The production methods for manzanilla and fino are essentially the same, and both types of sherry display a relatively low percentage of alcohol (15 to 17 percent), a pale straw color, and an underlying tangy flavor. The difference lies in where they are made and how the geography influences flavor and character. Both styles depend on the curious formation of *flor* on the surface of the wine in the cask, as well as the degree to which it forms. Manzanilla comes from the seaside town of Sanlúcar de Barrameda, where the crisp Atlantic breezes lend a distinct saline quality and a fresh, briny aroma that make the sherry a fine companion to such foods as fried seafood and olives. (In Spain, the nomenclature can be confusing since manzanilla is also the word for chamomile tea and for a small green olive that coincidentally pairs extremely well with this type of sherry.)

Fino is made farther inland, around the town of Jerez de la Frontera, and is the favorite and most consumed sherry in Spain. Finos are light, elegant wines that can also be quite complex, with a nose redolent of yeasty, freshly baked bread and a crisp, nutty flavor, making them a perfect complement to toasted and salted almonds and Spanish air-cured ham. Many aficionados consider fino sherry to be one of the greatest and most effective appetite stimulants in the wine-drinking world, preparing the palate for a range of foods to come. Both manzanillas and finos are fairly delicate due to their moderate alcohol level. They should be served chilled and consumed within a couple of days after opening.

Amontillado

This aromatic sherry falls into the fino category, and is really an aged, medium-bodied fino. The alcohol level is increased after its initial solera aging, and then the wine is transferred to another solera without the protective layer of *flor*, resulting in deeper hues gleaned both from the wood and the increased oxidation. Amontillados are almost always either dry or medium-dry, the latter due to the addition of the Pedro Ximénez grape. These sherries display a pronounced nuttiness, specifically the flavors of roasted hazelnuts and almonds. Amontillados should be served at cool cellar temperature.

Palo Cortado

This type of rare sherry nicely illustrates the unusual metamorphosis that these wines undergo. Considered a fino-type sherry, palo cortado begins life as a fino and then mysteriously casts off the mantle of *flor*, transforming itself into an amontillado. With more careful aging, another evolution occurs, and the sherry takes on the fuller body of an oloroso sherry. In other words, palo cortados are situated somewhere between amontillados and olorosos in terms of flavor, nose, and body. Serve these at cellar temperature.

Oloroso

Oloroso means fragrant in Spanish, an apt description for this type of sherry. New sherries that, for whatever reason, do not form a layer of *flor* are destined to become olorosos. Through oxidation and long aging in wood, they become rich, dark, nutty, velvety, and complex sherries, a perfect after-dinner drink. Olorosos, which can be very dry or can be sweetened with the addition of PX grapes, attain an alcohol content of about 18 percent. Serve them at room temperature.

Cream Sherry

This type of oloroso sherry, usually sweetened with PX and moscatel, gave rise to the image of sherry as a drink for little old ladies to sip in the parlor. In fact, cream sherries were originally created for the British export market and are not widely consumed in Spain. They range in sweetness from pleasant to cloying, and should be served as a digestive at room temperature.

Pedro Ximénez

In this form, the sherry really becomes more of a dessert than a drink. Normally only used to sweeten other types of palomino-based sherries, the PX grape flies solo here and can be as thick and rich as molasses. Not for the faint of heart, these sherries are usually poured over ice cream in Spain or served as a dessert wine at room temperature.

Sherries at César

Though it changes with time, this is the basic list of sherries that are available at César. They represent a spectrum of flavors and styles, from dry to sweet, and all of them are terrific with food.

Manzanilla, La Gitana, Hidalgo (fino)
Amontillado, Bodegas Dios Baco (semidry)
Amontillado, Principe, Barbadillo
Palo Cortado, Almacenista Vides 1/50, Lustau
Palo Cortado, Obispo Gascon, Barbadillo (very old)
Dry Oloroso, Cuco, Barbadillo
Dry Oloroso, Pata de Gallina, Almacenista Jarana 1/38, Lustau
Moscatel, Laura, Barbadillo (sweet)
Moscatel, Las Cruces, Lustau (sweet)
Oloroso, Del Tonel, Lustau (sweet)
Cream, Eva, Barbadillo (sweet)
Pedro Ximénez, Abuelo Diego 27, Montilla-Moriles, Alvear (very sweet)

Cocktails

César follows in a long line of traditional American saloons, bars, and cocktail lounges, and is infused with the spirit—and food—of the great tapas bars of Spain. We feel that this is a winning combination, for although Americans have always known how to drink, bar food in America has typically left much to be desired. Conversely, you would not usually find such an extensive selection of wine, spirits, and cocktails in the tapas bars of Spain. And just as we use only the best and freshest ingredients in our kitchen, we believe that a great cocktail can only be made when using high-quality, traditionally made spirits, flavorings, and mixers, and with techniques that present the drink at its most pristine, rather than a watered-down, pale imitation of itself.

All manner of theories have been put forth about the origin of cocktails—both the concept and the word itself—most asserting that "mixed" drinks arose in the nineteenth century. Cocktails as we know them, however, are strictly a twentieth-century American invention, having come into vogue during the Jazz Age, a time when style, elegance, and an insatiable thirst for alcohol swept the nation, the cinema, and subsequently the world. It also didn't hurt that ice was suddenly readily available, a must for the arctic-cold libations that were to fuel the jet set.

There are literally thousands of cocktail recipes out there, with more being invented all the time—so many that it would be impossible to catalog every one in a book. Many of today's drinks are variations on variations on variations of an original idea. Others are born simply out of the ingredients at hand, or to create a signature drink for a particular establishment. Still others were created to market a brand of liquor or to coincide with a special event. The fact is, there are hundreds of cocktails that are barely distinguishable from one another, and some that are just plain silly.

There are over fifty cocktail recipes in this book, all of which have been carefully chosen to represent what we consider the best drinks from each major spirit category. Many are César originals (marked with an asterisk); others are our interpretations of established classics. César's house tequila drink, the Three-Citrus Margarita—one of our variations on a classic—is an example of a subtle change adding a new dimension to a drink. And once you've tried a Chapala, why would you ever again make a Tequila Sunrise unless, heaven forbid, you run out of limes! The eight whiskey recipes represent a broad spectrum of flavors and are arguably the best uses for whiskey outside of sipping it straight, with or without ice. We like to think that one could derive an infinite amount of drinking pleasure from this list, never tiring of the selection.

At César, we have always looked for, and been blessed with, bartenders who have more going on than a list of recipes in their heads. A good bartender is a rare combination of scientist, alchemist, short-order cook, therapist, and entertainer. They must be able to work well and efficiently under a great deal of pressure; possess a singular knowledge of spirits, wines, and various cocktail aromatics (and be able to find them during the rush); and understand the subtle distinctions that differentiate a good drink from a bad one and, perhaps more importantly, a good one from a great one. In that spirit, these recipes are dedicated to all the talented mixologists who have plied their craft behind the bar at César, including Kathleen, Bill, Dennis, Richard, Olivier, Tim, Max, Pattiann, Michaela, and Farid.

Anatomy of a Cocktail

The cocktail recipes in this book are self-explanatory, but for those who have never mixed drinks before, or for those who have relied on cocktail mixes, here are some tips that will help you be a better bartender and, consequently, a better host. The most important rule of thumb is that your cocktails will only be as good as the ingredients you use. Always use good-quality spirits and mixers. This doesn't mean you have to use the twenty-five-year-old Macallan Scotch whisky for your Rob Roy (though it may be the best Rob Roy you've ever had); just avoid cut-rate, cheap liquor. As with cooking with wine, don't make cocktails with liquor that you wouldn't enjoy drinking straight. Be sensible, however, and consider the use of the liquor before choosing a brand. Many of the best and most expensive Scotch whiskies, though delicious on their own, would overpower any other flavoring in a cocktail, and therefore would not be the best choice despite their inherent quality. If you are new to the game, take notice at your favorite drinking establishments and see what liquors they use for their cocktails. Ask if you can try other brands and styles for the same drink, and decide which you prefer. That's the beauty of a bar: you can try all sorts of drinks without investing hundreds of dollars in liquor stock. Here are some other essential tips for bartending.

Essential Tips

Invest in proper glassware. At the very least, have martini glasses, highball glasses, and old-fashioned glasses. Additional glassware can include champagne flutes, single-shot vodka glasses, heat-tempered glass mugs, and brandy snifters.

With very few exceptions, cocktails should be served very cold. Avoid making a cocktail so large that it gets warm before it can be drunk.

Keep your martini glasses chilled, either in the freezer or on ice.

Use plenty of ice. It's the cheapest item in your bar, so don't skimp. With a few exceptions, liquor should be poured over ice, not the other way around. If you are shaking a drink but are still serving it on the rocks, strain the drink over fresh ice in the glass.

Never reuse ice in a shaker. When making a new drink, use fresh ice.

Don't leave liquor sitting on ice in the cocktail shaker while you do something else. When you start a drink, make sure you finish it right away.

Whenever possible, squeeze juice to order, especially lemon and lime juice. A handheld juice squeezer is perfect for smaller fruit and just as fast as pouring it out of a can.

For other juices, such as cranberry or pineapple, where squeezing to order is not practical, make sure it is freshly opened. If you have leftovers from your last party, discard them and start with fresh juice.

Use superfine sugar at the bar; it dissolves more quickly and completely than regular granulated sugar.

For twists, use a channel knife or stripper to peel a long, thin piece of the rind. If you do this over the glass, you will get a spritz of essential oils that will do more to flavor the drink than a dried-out twist cut hours before.

Be considerate of nondrinkers. Plan to have a selection of nonalcoholic beverages that are as interesting as the cocktails. These are not only for teetotalers, but also for designated drivers or anyone who feels he or she has had enough.

Use the proper amount of alcohol in a drink. Moderate drinking should mean fewer drinks, not weak ones. Ultimately, with the exception of the size, remember the immortal words of James Bond: "I never have more than one drink before dinner. But I do like that one to be large and very strong and very well made."

Simple syrups are a great way to add sweetness to a cocktail without the sugar clouding the drink. They are easy to make and keep indefinitely in a covered container. We call for them specifically in three cocktails in this book, but you can use simple syrups in place of sugar in most recipes. Note that when muddling is involved, superfine sugar works better than syrups.

Simple Syrup

1 cup water
1 cup sugar

Combine the water and sugar in a medium saucepan over high heat. Cook, stirring constantly, until the sugar dissolves and the mixture reaches a full boil. Remove from the heat and chill.

Mint Simple Syrup

Once the sugar water comes to a full boil, remove from the heat, add ½ bunch mint, and steep for 15 minutes. Strain and chill.

Lemon-Mint Simple Syrup

Make, steep, and strain the mint syrup as directed. Add 1 cup freshly squeezed lemon juice and chill.

Gin Classics

French 75

Gimlet

Gin Rickey

Negroni

Parisienne

Tom Collins

Despite its often dubious reputation (mothers' ruin, you know), gin is without doubt the quintessential cocktail liquor, an elegant, sophisticated component of a well-stocked modern bar. The Martini alone would secure gin's place in the pantheon of bar spirits, and when you consider such great drinks as the Negroni or the soothing sit-me-by-the-pool-and-leave-me-alone gin and tonic, one can easily see that gin is indispensable in any civilized bar.

Invented in Holland in the seventeenth century, gin was originally called "essence of *genièvre*" because of its distinctive juniper flavoring and was intended for medicinal purposes. The name evolved to Geneva and then to Genever, and then in English, after the British fell in love with the stuff, to gin. Gin's nefarious reputation is due in part to the vast quantities of bathtub varieties made during "the great experiment," Prohibition, and to the riotous consumption of inferior gin in England during the eighteenth century.

Gin starts life in much the same way as vodka or whiskey does, as a flavorless, clear distillate from various types of grain. It is in the addition of the botanicals, such as juniper and various herbs, that gin becomes gin. These ingredients are jealously kept secret by manufacturers, since they distinguish their gin from everyone else's. Gin owes nothing to *terroir* and could conceivably be made anywhere. Most of the best brands, though, are still made in England, with some notable ones coming from Holland and the United States. Gin's place at the bar is, of course, legendary. It plays fair and mixes well with others, but is not content to be pushed into the background by mixers, preferring instead to stand up and be noticed. And yet its ethereal, flowery bouquet is at times so subtle as to defy description. We continue to try, however, over a dry Martini. Here's looking at you, kid.

French 75

¾ ounce **gin**

Dash of **Simple Syrup** (page 17)

Dash of **grenadine**

¼ ounce freshly squeezed **lemon juice**

Chilled **Champagne** to fill

While we generally think that guns and alcohol should never be mixed, this drink happens to be named for a lightweight field gun used during World War I. But forget about that aspect of this cocktail's pedigree, and instead enjoy the inspired marriage of gin and Champagne. Who knew?

Combine the gin, syrup, grenadine, and lemon juice in a shaker with ice. Stir gently and strain into a champagne flute. Fill with Champagne.

Gimlet

1½ ounces **gin**

½ ounce freshly squeezed **lemon juice**

Splash of **Rose's Lime Juice**

Lime wedge, for garnish

The origin of the name is simple enough. A gimlet is a T-shaped tool with a screw tip, and in the days when wine, beer, and spirits were still transported and dispensed in wooden casks, the gimlet was used to bore the hole for the tap. The ingredients represent two longtime English favorites, gin and lime, a combination that kept scurvy at bay for many a "Limey" in the days when the sun never set on the British Empire. In fact, Rose's Lime Juice, a sweetened, concentrated lime juice, was developed in Scotland in the mid-nineteenth century and was sold to shipping companies for just that reason. Today, we drink Gimlets because they taste good. The addition of lemon brings a refreshing note and helps cut the sweetness of the Rose's Lime Juice.

Combine the gin, lemon juice, and lime juice in a shaker with ice, and shake well. Strain into a martini glass. Garnish with a lime wedge.

Gin Rickey

A close cousin of both the Collins and the Fizz, the Rickey is typically a very dry cocktail. Too dry in our opinion, hence the addition of a little sugar. It is allegedly named for Colonel Joe Rickey, an American lobbyist in Washington, D.C., in the late nineteenth century. Serve it as a refreshing alternative to a gin and tonic on a warm summer day.

Combine the gin, sugar, lime juice, and bitters in a shaker with ice, and pour back into a highball glass filled with ice. Fill with club soda and garnish with a lime wedge.

1½ ounces **gin**

1 teaspoon **superfine sugar**

Juice of 1 lime

2 dashes of **angostura bitters**

Club soda to fill

Lime wedge, for garnish

Negroni

This is one of the few classic cocktails to have been invented in Italy. Legend has it that when Count Negroni grew tired of his regular Americano, he asked for it to be livened up with the addition of gin. With a slight adjustment to the mix, basically excluding the soda water, the Negroni was born. A lovely drink before dinner, the Negroni's steely, no-nonsense, slightly bitter demeanor is usually well-suited to those for whom the Martini is too austere. The Negroni should be served straight up and very cold. Avoid shaking too hard, for the color of the drink should be bright and clear, reflecting the last afternoon rays of sun through the glass as you take your first sip.

Combine the gin, Campari, and vermouth in a shaker with ice, and shake gently. Strain into a martini glass. Using a bar stripper, slowly peel a long, thin orange twist over the glass, gently misting the surface with the fruit's essential oils, and leave it to drape languorously over the rim.

1 ounce **gin**

¾ ounce **Campari**

1 ounce **sweet vermouth**

Twist of orange, for garnish

Tom Collins

Parisienne

The origin of this drink is obscure, but the French connection no doubt has to do with Parisians' affinity for gin in the golden age of cocktails, as well as for the use of French vermouth and cassis. Also implied in the feminine suffix is that it was a ladies' drink. We just think it's a very smart aperitif, and that Paris is a state of mind.

Combine the gin, vermouth, and cassis in a shaker filled with ice. Stir and strain into a martini glass with an ice cube. Garnish with a twist of lemon.

¾ ounce **gin**

¾ ounce **Noilly Prat dry vermouth**

Dash of **crème de cassis**

Twist of lemon, for garnish

Tom Collins

The only difference between a Collins and a Fizz is in the garnish and the fact that the Fizz is first shaken before the addition of the soda. They are both variations on a sour. Named originally for Old Tom Gin (a sweet variety of London gin), the standard today is made with any brand of London dry gin. There are versions of a Collins for almost any type of spirit, but the most common ones today are the Tom Collins and his brother John Collins, made with whiskey, usually Bourbon. Along with a gin and tonic, this is the quintessential refresher on a hot summer's day.

Combine the gin, sugar, and lemon juice in a shaker with ice, and swizzle gently. Without shaking, strain into a highball glass with ice and fill with club soda. Garnish with a lemon slice and a maraschino cherry.

1½ ounces **gin**

1 teaspoon **superfine sugar**

1 ounce freshly squeezed **lemon juice**

Club soda to fill

Lemon slice and **maraschino cherry**, for garnish

Martini

César Martini*

Venetian Martini*

Cortini*

Sherry Martini*

Chocolate Martini*

*César original

The Martini

So much has been written about the Martini one might think it was invented by the ancient Egyptians themselves. Countless bartenders, towns and decades have been credited with its invention, and we believe all of them. It really matters little who first created the Martini, though, because the drink has evolved considerably over the century or so of its existence, to the point that its true inventor would hardly recognize it.

To many drinkers, the Martini is the ultimate cocktail, a lean, clean, austere quaff that bites at the senses and piques the appetite before dinner, or before another Martini. Since the middle of the twentieth century, it has become increasingly dry, meaning that it is made with less and less vermouth to the point of obsession (one quipster said that he mixes his Martini while glancing at a picture of the inventor of vermouth). There are bartenders of repute who employ eyedroppers, misters, and other spartan apparatuses to administer the vermouth as though they were mixing rocket fuel (come to think of it, they are).

We believe that vermouth should be used in a Martini, albeit sparingly, and that it should be part of the mix, not merely spritzed on the surface. A good Martini—whether made with gin or vodka—should also be very cold and shaken well, so that barely perceivable shards of ice float on the surface, which are ideally consumed before they disappear. Think of these shards as the canary in the mine shaft: if they have melted, the drink is already too warm. In other words, a Martini must be consumed at once. To allow it to languish on the bar, becoming a tepid, flaccid reflection of its former self, is a crime against mixology. In this regard, the current trend toward huge Martinis is rather absurd. You can't drink them fast enough to keep them from getting warm unless you have the capacity of W. C. Fields. Herein we offer six versions of the Martini that we serve regularly at César to some very discriminating Martini drinkers.

"The subtle difference between the firm motion of shaking a proper Martini and the gentle coaxing of a Negroni distinguish a good bartender from a great one."

Martini-Shaking

The skills involved in shaking a cocktail are perhaps the most important aspect of a bartender's training. The subtle difference between the firm motion of shaking a proper Martini and the gentle coaxing of a Negroni distinguish a good bartender from a great one. Early in the classic film *The Thin Man,* William Powell instructs a line of bartenders in the proper techniques of mixology, telling them, "A Manhattan you shake to the fox-trot, and a Bronx to a two-step time. But the dry Martini you always shake to waltz time." At César, we take the training of our bartenders very seriously. In that spirit, we asked nuclear physicist and César patron Ed Morse to catalog the meticulous science of shaking the proper cocktail.

1. Angle to horizontal plane must be maintained at 37.28° ± 0.6°.

2. All applicable OSHA and EPA codes apply to unintentional or intentional misuse of substances contained within shaking vessel and to body extension required of bartender during shaking operation.

3. Care must be taken not to injure customer and/or other staff during shaking phase.

4. All operators of shaking device must complete vigorous training course (conducted in broken French).

5. Axial acceleration applied to shaking device must be controlled to within ± 0.05 g for specific conditions of drink.

6. Shaking device must be 18/8 stainless steel, type 302 or 304, thickness 20 mil or greater. Periodic inspection of shaking device is mandatory.

7. Retaining cup should be restaurant size #23 pint glass, borosilicate type, wall thickness 0.105 inch with a minimum base thickness of 0.25 inch. Retaining cup should not have cracks or other flaws.

8. Motion of device should not exceed 45 seconds unless operator signs waiver with management, releasing it from responsibility for repetitive-stress injury claims.

9. Operator of shaking device should periodically test product for quality and consistency and make adjustments to above motional specification to produce product of highest possible quality.

10. Shake responsibly.

Martini

Splash of **dry vermouth**

2 ounces **gin** or **vodka**

Cocktail olive, twist of lemon, or **caperberry** (see page 86), for garnish

Here we offer three versions of the classic Martini: dry, not so dry, and downright wet. As for garnish, many insist on the traditional olive, while others prefer a twist of lemon, especially with a vodka Martini, or a whole caperberry. Still others opt for no garnish at all. You decide.

For a dry Martini, pour a splash of vermouth into a martini glass and swirl to coat. Discard the excess. Place the gin in a shaker with ice, and shake well. Strain over the desired garnish in the glass.

For a slightly less dry version, combine the vermouth and gin in a shaker with ice and shake well. Strain over the desired garnish in the glass.

For a wet Martini, combine a ratio of 1 part dry vermouth to 2 parts gin in a shaker with ice, and shake well. Strain over the desired garnish in the glass.

César Martini

Splash of **pastis**

1½ ounces **vodka**

The intense licorice flavor makes this an inspired aperitif— a clean, piercing drink that tingles the senses and stimulates the taste buds.

Pour a splash of pastis into a martini glass. Place the vodka in a shaker with ice, and shake well. Strain into the glass.

Martini

Venetian Martini

1½ ounces **gin**

½ ounce **Carpano Antica Formula**
(a sweet Italian vermouth)

Twist of orange, for garnish

This version harks back to the first Martini recipes to appear in print at the end of the nineteenth century. They called for Old Tom (a sweet English gin), sweet vermouth, and orange bitters. This modern, more restrained mix still leans toward the sweet side. Drink it with someone you love (that could be yourself).

Combine the gin and vermouth in a shaker with ice, and shake well. Strain into a martini glass and garnish with a twist of orange.

Cortini

Lemon wedge

1½ ounces **Old Raj gin**

Sacramento wine and food importer Darrel Corti was the inspiration for this drink. Although you can make it with any brand of gin, we specifically recommend Old Raj brand because of its singular nature. It is a viscous liquor, very fragrant, with a yellowish tinge (due to the inclusion of saffron) that is complemented nicely by the lemon.

Put the lemon wedge—without squeezing—and the gin in a shaker with ice, and shake well. Strain into a martini glass.

Sherry Martini

Depending on the brand and type of sherry used (see pages 9–11), this drink can vary from very dry (fino) to sweet and rich (oloroso), and everything in between. In other words, you can have it as an aperitif or as an after-dinner sweet with dessert, kicked up a notch with the vodka.

1½ ounces **vodka**

½ ounce **fino** or **amontillado sherry**

Combine the vodka and sherry in a shaker with ice, and shake well. Strain into a martini glass.

Chocolate Martini

When you consider how sweet the original Martinis were, this version is not so far-fetched. Enjoy it at brunch, as a late afternoon pick-me-up, or as a fun after-dinner drink—with or without dessert.

1 ounce **vodka**

1 ounce **Godiva liqueur**

½ ounce **vanilla liqueur**

Combine the vodka and liqueurs in a shaker with ice, and shake gently. Strain into a martini glass.

For variations on the Chocolate Martini, try replacing the vanilla liqueur with either green crème de menthe or Mandarine Napoleon brandy.

Vodka

César Cosmopolitan

Kamikaze

Lemon Drop

Madras

Marius*

Mudslide

Salty Dog

Sea Breeze

Sorrento*

White Russian

*César original

White Russian

By its very definition, and even according to the U.S. government, vodka is supposed to be a colorless, tasteless, odorless alcoholic beverage, devoid of any discernable character. However, anyone who has ever tasted several different vodkas at one sitting knows that that definition is correct in only one particular—vodka is indeed colorless. As for the rest, good vodkas—actually even bad vodkas—have noticeable differences in mouth feel, aroma, and flavor, subtle though they may be.

Vodka means "little water" in Russian, the diminutive form of *zhiznennia voda,* or "water of life." Unlike eau-de-vie in France, vodka is made from grain, such as wheat, barley, or rye, or in rare cases from potatoes. It wasn't a very popular spirit in the United States until sometime in the 1950s, when it was successfully sold via Madison Avenue to the American public.

While there are connoisseurs who enjoy vodka for the pure sensual pleasure it provides, its main popularity stems from the fact that when mixed with juices or strong sodas, it virtually disappears. In other words, it is the perfect alcohol for those who don't like alcohol. Nevertheless, when mixed properly there should be some semblance of the spirit left in the glass to enjoy, and therefore it stands to reason that a better-quality vodka will produce a better drink.

Vodka is hands-down the most popular spirit in America today, and it figures in some of our most cherished cocktails. It even rivals gin as the preferred Martini base in bars across the land, so much so that traditionalists usually have to specify if they want the latter. Let's not overlook the fact that vodka is perhaps the quintessential accompaniment to caviar, and that a bottle of the good stuff in the freezer is a welcome friend. Plenty of top-shelf vodkas are readily available today, one or two of which are even made in the States, and we urge you to try them all. After all, 150 million Russians can't be wrong. To that we say, *noz drovya!*

César Cosmopolitan

1 1/2 ounces **Absolut Mandrin vodka**

1/4 ounce **Cointreau**

3/4 ounce freshly squeezed **lime juice**

1/2 ounce **cranberry juice**

Lime slice, for garnish

The Cosmopolitan has quickly become a modern classic, no doubt spurred on by its appealing color as well as by its sophisticated moniker. Like its cousin, the Lemon Drop (page 36), this drink should never be cloyingly sweet, but should refresh and dance lightly on the palate. Despite—or perhaps because of—its popularity among women, many men still have an aversion to this fancy cocktail (real men don't drink pink drinks). So to all the ladies and self-confident men out there, cheers!

Combine the vodka, Cointreau, lime juice, and cranberry juice in a shaker with ice, and shake well. Strain into a martini glass. Garnish with a lime slice.

Kamikaze

1 1/2 ounces **vodka**

1/2 ounce **Cointreau**

1/2 ounce freshly squeezed **lime juice**

1/2 ounce **Rose's Lime Juice**

Lime wedge, for garnish

The original version of this drink, calling for a full jigger of vodka and a splash of Rose's Lime Juice, was intended as a shot to get one drunk, or at least a good buzz, quickly. Our modern recipe is more on the order of a vodka sour, meant to be sipped and savored. However, if you find yourself going off to battle, the original might be in order.

Combine the vodka, Cointreau, and lime juices in a shaker with ice, and shake well. Strain into a martini glass and garnish with a lime wedge.

Cosmopolitan

Lemon Drop

Superfine sugar, for coating rim of glass

1½ ounces **Hangar One "Buddha's Hand" Citron** or **Ketel One Citroen vodka**

½ ounce **Cointreau**

½ ounce freshly squeezed **lemon juice**

Twist of lemon, for garnish

In a relatively short time, this drink has established itself as a modern classic; it's so new that it rarely appears in cocktail books. Essentially, the Lemon Drop is another variation on a sour. We have suggested a couple of specific vodkas because they are our favorites among the lemon-flavored varieties, and because one is made in our own backyard. Hangar One is crafted at an old military structure in Alameda, California, by two artisanal distillers. Be careful not to make this drink too sweet; it should be refreshing, not candy.

Coat the rim of a chilled martini glass with sugar. Combine the vodka, Cointreau, and lemon juice in a shaker with ice, and shake well. Strain into the glass, and garnish with a twist of lemon.

Madras

1½ ounces **vodka**

Freshly squeezed **orange juice**

Cranberry juice

Think of this as a cross between a Sea Breeze and a Tequila Sunrise. It is a refreshing, easy-to-drink highball that lives or dies by the quality and freshness of the orange juice. Find the sweetest oranges you can, and juice them as needed.

Pour the vodka into a highball glass over ice. Fill with equal parts orange juice and cranberry juice.

Lemon Drop

Marius

1½ ounces **vodka**

¼ ounce **crème de cassis**

Juice of ½ **lemon**

Twist of lemon, for garnish

In the delightful film trilogy that inspired César's name, Marius is the son of César who runs off to sea, leaving behind the quayside bar in which he was raised. The taste of the black currants may evoke memories of the popular Provençal Kir (white wine with a splash of crème de cassis). Think of this delicious aperitif as a Kir on steroids.

Combine the vodka, crème de cassis, and lemon juice in a shaker with ice, and shake well. Strain into a martini glass, and garnish with a twist of lemon.

Mudslide

¾ ounce **vodka**

¾ ounce **Baileys Irish Cream**

¾ ounce **Kahlúa**

This luscious, dessertlike drink was no doubt invented in one of California's coastal communities where they know about such things, but it can be enjoyed in the flatlands as well. Note the similarity to a White Russian, but the Mudslide is richer and fudgier.

Fill an old-fashioned glass three-fourths full with ice. Pour in the vodka, Baileys, and Kahlúa, and serve.

Salty Dog

Kosher salt, for coating rim of glass

1½ ounces **vodka**

Freshly squeezed **grapefruit juice** to fill

Cousin to the Greyhound and the Sea Breeze, the Salty Dog represents vodka in its most relaxed and casual attire. It is really just a Greyhound with a salted rim. Leave off the salt and add a splash of cranberry juice and you have a Sea Breeze. Any way you pour it, however, this is a great restorative after a long day.

Coat the rim of a highball glass with salt. Fill three-fourths full with ice. Pour in the vodka, and fill with grapefruit juice.

Sea Breeze

This is a Greyhound with a splash of cranberry juice. To confuse matters further, if you omit the grapefruit juice, you have a Cape Codder.

Pour the vodka into a highball glass over ice. Fill with equal parts grapefruit juice and cranberry juice.

1½ ounces **vodka**

Freshly squeezed **grapefruit juice** to fill

Cranberry juice to fill

Sorrento

Evoking images of the breathtaking Amalfi coast in southern Italy, and Sorrento in particular, this drink is a tribute to the vibrant flavor of the lemons for which the town is justly famous. Lemon takes center stage here in the form of the singular liqueur from the region. (Why is it spelled with the English "lemon" and not the Italian "limone"? It just is.) Drink one and imagine you see the Isle of Capri off in the distance. After two, perhaps you will.

Pour the lemoncello into a martini glass. Place the vodka in a shaker with ice, and shake well. Strain into the glass, and garnish with a twist of lime.

½ ounce **lemoncello**

1½ ounces **vodka**

Twist of lime, for garnish

White Russian

A Black Russian is simply vodka and Kahlúa, and is one of the few cocktails not invented in the United States (reportedly it was created at the bar at the Hôtel Métropole in Brussels). With the addition of cream on top, it becomes a lovely after-dinner drink, perhaps as an alternative to dessert.

Pour the vodka and Kahlúa into an old-fashioned glass over ice. Gently pour the cream over the top. Do not stir, leaving the option to the imbiber.

1 ounce **vodka**

¾ ounce **Kahlúa**

1 ounce **heavy cream**

Whiskey

Lucky 13*

Manhattan

Mint Julep

Old Fashioned

Rob Roy

Rusty Nail

Sazerac

Whiskey Sour

César original

Old Fashioned

Americans can't lay claim to much in the realm of original spirits, even though we certainly produce and consume our fair share. However, one distillate that is unique to our side of the Atlantic is Bourbon, that sweet, vanilla-laden, predominantly corn-based whiskey* named for a county in Kentucky that ironically is now dry (as in no booze allowed).

Whiskey has always been a popular spirit in the States, from cowpokes who liked their red-eye straight to modern urbanites who sip Manhattans and single malts in café society. The name comes from the Gaelic term *uisge beatha,* which evolved into *usque baugh* (pronounced OOS-keh baw), both translating to "water of life."

Whiskey was born when the art of distillation was brought to the Celtic islands by thirsty monks. (Tippling friars were responsible for most of the alcoholic beverages we enjoy today.) It is made from grain that is cooked in great amounts of water to release the essential sugars, then mixed with yeast and fermented, ending up in its initial stage exactly like beer. In fact, most whiskey distillers refer to the predistilled liquid as such (suddenly a Boilermaker—a shot of whiskey followed by a beer—makes sense). The liquid is then carefully distilled, often repeatedly, and finally put up in oak barrels to age, from which it derives its color and much of its flavor.

The barrels themselves are a source of much debate among distillers. The Scots insist on used Bourbon barrels (they joke that the Bourbon industry exists to prepare the barrels for the making of Scotch whisky; we are not amused) or barrels that have been used to make sherry or port. The American distillers prefer new oak that has been charred by fire. The Scottish distillers further enhance the flavor of the spirit by drying the malted (germinated) grain over peat fires, resulting in the trademark smokiness that is anathema to Bourbon drinkers but highly regarded by Scotch lovers.

At César, we stock a wide range of Scotch single-malt whiskies (malted whiskies from a single distillery) from all the great regions of Scotland. The styles range from delicately smoky, lightly colored whisky to huge powerhouses full of smoke and leather. In fact, we offer whiskies from all the major producing countries (Scotland, Ireland, Canada, Japan, and the United States) in the belief that the spirit deserves an exalted place at the bar. In its many guises, whiskey is responsible for some of the world's great cocktails, as well as for inspiring a cult following for its finer sipping varieties. We are pleased to share our versions of some of the classic whiskey cocktails. Here's mud in your eye!

Note: "Whiskey" is the spelling used by most American and Irish distillers, while "whisky" is the spelling used by the Scots, Canadians, and more recently by the Japanese.

Lucky 13

1 ounce **Hirsch 13-year-old rye whiskey** or similar aged rye

½ ounce **Carpano Antica Formula** (a sweet Italian vermouth)

Dash of **angostura bitters**

Maraschino cherry, for garnish

Why lucky? Maybe it's the thirteen years that Hirsch rye whiskey spends maturing in oak casks. Or maybe we're all just lucky to have such a good-tasting drink. This take on the classic Manhattan is smooth and sweet, with a hint of smokiness from the rye adding interesting dimension and character. Stir this drink gently; it should be cold but remain a clear, dark amber.

Combine the whiskey, vermouth, and bitters in a shaker with ice, and stir gently. Strain over a maraschino cherry in a martini glass.

Manhattan

1½ ounces **whiskey**, preferably **Bourbon**

¾ ounce **sweet vermouth**

2 or 3 dashes of **angostura bitters**

Maraschino cherry, for garnish

Among serious cocktail drinkers, the world is divided neatly in half: those for whom the Martini is the ultimate in elegant, sophisticated, predinner quaffs, and those who gladly say, "I'll take Manhattan." Easily the most famous among the family of whiskey cocktails, the Manhattan boasts virtues that have been extolled by bon viveurs *from F. Scott Fitzgerald to James Villas, who claimed that it "represents the height of the mixologist's art." Properly made, it is a delicate balance between the sweet and the bitter, both of which serve to modify the whiskey. Always choose a good Bourbon or rye rather than a blended whiskey, for while the interplay between the vermouth and bitters is crucial, it should never overwhelm the whiskey. A note about the nomenclature: There is a classic Manhattan (always made with sweet vermouth), a dry Manhattan (made with dry vermouth), and a perfect Manhattan (a combination of sweet and dry vermouth). There is no such thing as a sweet Manhattan, as that would be redundant. As for the garnish, the maraschino cherry is an integral part of the classic, rather than merely a decoration, though you may choose to eat it or not. A dry Manhattan takes a twist of lemon, and a perfect Manhattan can take either.*

Combine the whiskey, vermouth, and bitters in a shaker with ice, and stir gently; the idea is to make it cold but not foamy. Strain over a maraschino cherry in a martini glass.

Manhattan

Mint Julep

Mint Julep

A sure sign of a classic cocktail is the amount of controversy it evokes concerning how it should properly be made. The Mint Julep indeed qualifies. In this case, the debate revolves around what to do with the mint—to crush or not to crush. Far be it from a bunch of Yankees to attempt to define this most southern of cocktails, and the official quaff of the Kentucky Derby, the annual race that is to horse racing aficionados what the Super Bowl is to football fans (except the Super Bowl doesn't have its own cocktail, unless you count the six-pack). Derbyites insist that the mint is there to create a subtle bouquet, an aroma to be enjoyed while sipping the Julep, rather than a flavor component of the drink itself. To this end, eminent bartender and spirits authority Gary Regan recommends using a bunch of mint as garnish spilling over the rim, along with short straws that cause the drinker to bury his or her nose in the mint while drinking. However, should you find yourself wanting a Mint Julep on one of the other 364 non-Derby days of the year, and you wish to intensify the mintiness of the drink, try our version that includes a splash of easy-to-make mint syrup. This drink is best enjoyed while rocking on someone's front porch on a hot, sunny afternoon.

1 ounce **Mint Simple Syrup** (page 17)

2 ounces **Bourbon**

Several **mint sprigs,** chopped or cut up with a scissors

Pour the syrup and bourbon into an old-fashioned glass and stir. Almost fill the glass with crushed ice. Pack the mint leaves on top of the ice. Use a short straw or no straw at all.

Old Fashioned

½ teaspoon **superfine sugar** or 1 **sugar cube**

2 dashes **angostura bitters**

½ **orange slice**

Maraschino cherry

1½ ounces **whiskey**

Club soda to fill

The name of this venerable cocktail implies that it's been around for a long time, which it has, but why it was so named in the first place no one really knows for sure. What we do know is that it is a darn good drink, especially for those who like their whiskey softened around the edges and a tad sweet. Most classic versions call for blended whiskey, but we believe it is enhanced by using a good Bourbon. You decide. When mashing the fruit, avoid crushing the orange peel, as the bitter tannins in the peel will be released. Olivier likes to use bar sugar, and Kathleen Ventura, our first (and maybe best) bartender, prefers a sugar cube. It's up to you. In the end, what more can be said about a drink that has its own glass named for it, except try it and see for yourself.

Place the sugar in an old-fashioned glass, then pour the bitters on top of it. Add the orange and cherry and mash strongly with a muddler, taking care not to crush the orange peel too much. Add the whiskey and some ice. Fill with club soda.

Rob Roy

1½ ounces **Scotch whisky**

¾ ounce **sweet vermouth**

2 dashes of **angostura bitters**

Maraschino cherry, for garnish

Robert Macgregor, the eighteenth-century Scottish freedom fighter for whom this drink is named, probably never partook of its pleasure, though he no doubt took his share of whisky. Roy is a Scottish nickname for a man with red hair, an apt description of this cocktail. The drink is basically a Scotch Manhattan, with the Scotch lending a subtle smoky element to the mix.

Combine the Scotch, vermouth, and bitters in a shaker with ice, and stir gently; the drink should remain clear. Strain over a maraschino cherry in a martini glass.

Rusty Nail

This simple digestive combines two of Scotland's greatest exports, the singular liqueur Drambuie and the whisky from which it is derived. Don't stir this drink; instead let the whisky be pulled up through the liqueur floating on top.

Pour the Scotch and then the Drambuie into an old-fashioned glass over ice.

1 ounce **Scotch whisky**
½ ounce **Drambuie**

Sazerac

Certain names in the drinking world are the stuff of legends. This drink was named for the bar in New Orleans that concocted it, and the bar itself was named after the French brandy that was the drink's main ingredient. The original recipe calls for Sazerac brandy, along with absinthe and Peychaud bitters, the latter named for the nineteenth-century New Orleans apothecary who invented them (and who, incidentally, was known for serving brandy tonics in little egg cups, or coquêtiers, *which some have speculated are the genesis of the word "cocktail"). Over time whiskey replaced the brandy, and the less lethal pastis supplanted the absinthe. If all this is too confusing, just sit back and enjoy our version of this New Orleans classic.*

Pour a splash of pastis into a martini glass and swirl to coat. Discard the excess. Combine the Bourbon, bitters, and sugar in a shaker with ice, and shake well. Strain into the martini glass, and garnish with a twist of lemon.

Splash of **pastis**
2 ounces **Bourbon**
2 dashes of **angostura bitters**
½ teaspoon **superfine sugar**
Twist of lemon, for garnish

Whiskey Sour

1½ ounces **Bourbon**

½ ounce freshly squeezed **lemon juice**

½ teaspoon **superfine sugar**

Maraschino cherry, for garnish

Often overlooked and underappreciated, the Whiskey Sour was once a very popular cocktail. Its reputation was tarnished by too many versions made with the ubiquitous sour mix shot from bartenders' beverage guns and by cheap whiskey. Technically, a sour can be made from any spirit, but it is with whiskey that it achieves the greatest result because whiskey tends not to be eclipsed by the sweet and sour elements. For those of you who thought the Whiskey Sour went out with fins on a Cadillac, try this version for a very pleasant surprise, and resist all temptations to use a bottled mix.

Combine the Bourbon, lemon juice, and sugar in a shaker with ice, and shake moderately. Strain over a maraschino cherry in a martini glass.

Rum

Caipirinha
Cuban Manhattan*
Daiquiri
Cassis Daiquiri*
Mint Daiquiri*
Mojito
Rum Cocktail
Rum Starter
Rum Toddy
César original

Mojito

Just as gin was once the scourge of London, rum's early reputation was as the preferred drink of pirates, scalawags, and others of ill repute throughout the Caribbean, where it originated and where the vast majority of it is still made. The art of distilling came early to the colonies of the New World, emerging in the north as whiskey, in Mexico as tequila, and throughout the Caribbean islands in the form of rum.

Rum's origins are somewhat shrouded. No one even knows exactly how it got its name. Perhaps it came from rumbullion or rumbustious, both descriptions of the unruly behavior of those who imbibe; or perhaps it came from *saccharum,* Latin for "sugar," the prolific tropical reed from which rum is made and that was first brought to the area by Columbus himself. Or, as one authority surmises, it might simply have come from the British colloquialism "rum," meaning a jolly good thing.

Once the production of sugar and molasses got under way in the Caribbean, the plantation owners no doubt decided it was easier to transport casks of rum than the precarious and volatile molasses, not to mention the fact that it was more fun to sample during the long ocean voyages. These early shipments of rum from the islands back to the various mother countries further established it as the drink of choice for seafaring folk. Until recently, rum was still considered a daily ration for British sailors.

For most cocktail drinkers today, rum conjures images of sun and sand, fresh fruit and good times. Rum is Carnavale, colorful costumes, and lively dance. Rum is sexy. It is also the base spirit for an assortment of excellent cocktails, two of which, the Mojito and the Caipirinha, have been enjoying a renaissance of late.

At César, we take great delight in our assortment of rums, from the light, spirited clear rums for mixing to the deep, dark varieties that are the color of molasses, meant to be sipped on deck as the sun slips over the yardarm. Rum may just be the quintessential party spirit. Intensely aromatic, and versatile enough to stand with the most flavorful of mixers, it can wear a black tie, Hawaiian shirts, or no shirts at all. Rumbustiousness never tasted so good.

Caipirinha

1 **lime**, cut into 8 wedges

2 teaspoons **superfine sugar**

2 ounces **cachaça** (Brazilian rum)

The name implies the humble origins of this unique Brazilian drink— caipira *means "farmer" or "peasant" in Portuguese—and it was no doubt thirsty sugarcane growers who devised it from ingredients they would have had at hand. Despite its roots, the Caipirinha has become something of a cosmopolitan drink, and an absolute must for celebrating Carnavale, or most anything else for that matter.*

Place the lime wedges and sugar in an old-fashioned glass. Crush the lime to release its juice, and muddle to dissolve the sugar and blend it with the lime. Pour in the *cachaça* and stir to dissolve the sugar completely. Top with crushed ice.

Cuban Manhattan

1½ ounces **Flor de Cana rum**

½ ounce **sweet vermouth**

Dash of **angostura bitters**

Maraschino cherry, for garnish

This is a tropical rendition of the classic Manhattan cocktail. Flor de Cana is a wonderful gold rum from Nicaragua that we think makes a delightfully dry Manhattan, perfect for those who don't favor the sweetness of the regular version.

Combine the rum, vermouth, and bitters in a shaker with ice, and shake gently. Strain over a maraschino cherry in a martini glass.

Caipirinha

Daiquiri

Superfine sugar, for coating
rim of glass

1½ ounces **white rum**

½ teaspoon **superfine sugar**

Juice of ½ **lime**

Lime slice, for garnish

One of the most famous of all rum-based drinks, the Daiquiri is named after a small fishing village on the west coast of Cuba, presumably near where it was first devised. Legend has it that an American mining engineer working in Cuba at the turn of the last century invented the drink when guests were coming and he ran out of gin (a brass plaque so commemorates the feat in the Daiquiri Lounge at the Washington Army and Navy Club). Like the Caipirinha, however, it seems likely that the native Cubans were already dressing up their rum with the commonly available lime and sugar. Whoever thought it up, it's a fine drink for hot days and an even better one for hot nights.

Coat the rim of a martini glass with sugar. Combine the rum, sugar, and lime juice in a shaker with ice, and shake well. Strain into the glass, and garnish with a lime slice.

Cassis Daiquiri

Superfine sugar, for coating
rim of glass

1½ ounces **white rum**

½ ounce **crème de cassis**

Juice of ½ **lime**

This variation was developed by one of our newer bartenders, Tim Kampa. The crème de cassis provides the sweetener for a lusher, more full-bodied version of the classic Cuban cocktail.

Coat the rim of a martini glass with sugar. Combine the rum, crème de cassis, and lime juice in a shaker with ice, and shake well. Strain into the glass and garnish with a lime slice.

Mint Daiquiri

The addition of mint takes the Daiquiri to a whole new level, and the Cointreau adds another layer of fruity sweetness. Tim, one of our bartenders, calls this version a Mojito Manhattan. A most soothing drink.

Combine the rum, Cointreau, lime juice, sugar, and mint leaves in a shaker with ice, and shake gently. Strain into a cocktail glass and garnish with a sprig of mint.

2 ounces **white rum**

¼ ounce **Cointreau**

Juice of ½ **lime**

1 teaspoon **superfine sugar**

Handful of **mint leaves**

Mint sprig, for garnish

Mojito

Along with the Daiquiri, this is the national cocktail of Cuba, and it is getting to be as well known here in the States. Technique is everything in the Mojito. It is important that when muddling the mint you don't crush the leaves completely because doing so will release bitter juices. And since we believe in tradition, it is also important to drink it while looking up. Don't ask, just do it.

Combine the mint leaves, lime juice, and sugar in a highball glass. Gently muddle the mint leaves, lightly crushing them. Add the rum and stir to dissolve the sugar completely. Fill the glass with crushed ice, and add club soda to fill.

8 to 10 **mint leaves**

Juice of ½ **lime**

1½ teaspoons **superfine sugar**

2 ounces **white rum**

Club soda to fill

Rum Cocktail

Though not the most original of names, this is a colorful and sweet drink for those who prefer to sit and sip.

Pour the rum, Cointreau, grenadine, and lemon juice into an old-fashioned glass over ice. Stir and garnish with a lime wedge and a maraschino cherry.

1½ ounces **white rum**

Dash of **Cointreau**

Dash of **grenadine**

¾ ounce freshly squeezed **lemon juice**

Lime wedge and **maraschino cherry**, for garnish

Rum Starter

Think of this as an über-Daiquiri, a little something to get things going after a hard day or, as they do in Jamaica, to get the engines started after a hard night. Not a drink to linger over.

Pour the rum, sugar, and lime juice into a short glass or shot glass. No ice, no garnish. Just swirl, drink, and pray.

1 ounce **white rum**

1 teaspoon **superfine sugar**

¾ ounce freshly squeezed **lime juice**

Rum Toddy

This will cure what ails you, whether that happens to be a cold or a down-turn in the stock market. It must be served in a heat-tempered glass in order to prevent cracking; a glass coffee mug works well.

Combine the rum, honey, and lemon wedge in a heatproof glass, giving the lemon wedge a squeeze. Fill with just-off-the-stove boiled water.

1½ ounces **dark rum**

1 teaspoon **honey**

Lemon wedge

Boiling water to fill

Tequila & Mezcal

Chapala
Margarita
Three-Citrus Margarita*
Mezcal Sour

*César original

Margarita

Tequila!" goes the song, the very sound of which evokes images ranging from dusty western towns in old John Ford movies (it was John Wayne's favorite drink) to modern gringo bars featuring a rainbow of flavored Margaritas. Tequila's rise to prominence in recent years is nothing short of astounding, as top-shelf, carefully aged examples can rival single-malt whiskies in price and flavor. Nonetheless, tequila, and its somewhat unruly and unsupervised uncle, mezcal, are old—probably the oldest spirits made in the New World. The Aztecs were drinking pulque—a fermented beverage made from the sap that flows abundantly from the agave plant, and the basis for tequila—centuries before the civilization was plundered by the conquistadores. The Spanish applied a little European distillation know-how, and a new spirit was born.

Tequila takes its name from a town in the Mexican state of Jalisco. To be called tequila, it must be made from 100 percent blue agave and must be triple distilled. The difference between tequila and mezcal? It's like the relationship between Bourbon and whiskey: all tequila is mezcal, but not all mezcal is tequila.

Mezcal is made outside of the designated area of production for tequila, and can be made from other types of agave. It is mezcal that gained the reputation for having a worm inside the bottle, although that is rarely done these days and is not necessarily a sign of quality. Mezcal can be very good, however—sometimes as good as tequila itself, despite the many backyard versions made throughout Mexico—and in recent years it has been getting its due.

Although on its home turf tequila is more often consumed straight, it was through the now ubiquitous Margarita that it won the affection of the American public, starting in the 1950s. Today, no well-equipped bar is without an assortment of tequilas, from white or silver (plata) varieties bottled without any aging in wood, to gold (reposado) tequilas that have been aged in redwood casks, to añejo or aged versions that can sit in oak barrels for one to three years or more. While the oldest and best tequilas are meant for sipping, they can also be used to make outstanding, albeit expensive, cocktails. Here, then, are our versions of some classic tequila drinks.

Chapala

1½ ounces **tequila**

Freshly squeezed **orange juice** to fill

Juice of ½ **lime**

Splash of **grenadine**

This is a version of the ever popular Tequila Sunrise, but with the inspired addition of fresh lime juice. A refreshing and relatively healthful drink, it's perfect for the first cocktail on a lazy afternoon, or for the last one as you watch the first red streaks of sunrise with someone you love.

Pour the tequila, orange juice, and lime juice into a highball glass over ice. Pour the contents, including the ice, into a shaker and then back into the glass without agitating the mixture too much. Pour the grenadine into the glass carefully, letting it slowly seep down through the drink. Do not stir.

Margarita

Kosher salt, for coating rim of glass

1½ ounces **tequila**

1 ounce freshly squeezed **lime juice**

½ ounce **Cointreau** or **triple sec**

Lime slice, for garnish

More than one woman has been credited with the inspiration for this drink, and to echo the sentiments of one wise bartender we know, bless each and every one of them. Whoever Margarita was, she left a marvelous legacy: this is one of the all-time great cocktails. Margarita drinkers are divided as to whether the drink should be served straight up or on the rocks, or made using the modern method of pouring it all into a blender for a frozen version. Since we don't use blenders at César, we eschew that last version altogether. Controversy also abounds as to whether lemon or lime is the correct fruit, or whether a combination is best. After much experimentation, we believe lime works the best, and in a pinch, we use a little of each (see the Three-Citrus Margarita). Whichever you choose (and we encourage comparison tasting), make sure the juice is freshly squeezed and that you use good tequila.

Coat the rim of a martini glass (for straight up) or an old-fashioned glass (on the rocks) with salt. Combine the tequila, lime juice, and Cointreau in a shaker with ice. Shake well if serving straight up, moderately if on the rocks. Strain into the glass, and garnish with a lime slice.

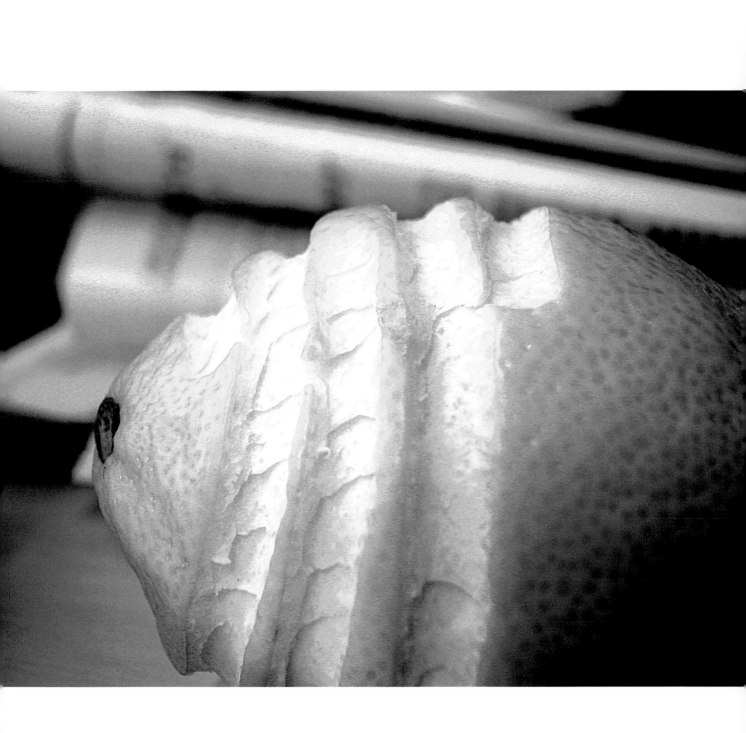

Three-Citrus Margarita

Three-Citrus Margarita

Classics are often hard to improve on, but here is an exception. Developed by one of our bartenders, Farid Dormishian, it may well be the ultimate Margarita. The additional citrus notes, plus the subtle taste of the crème de cassis, give this cocktail new depths of flavor and make it oh, so refreshing. The level of sweetness can be adjusted simply by stirring the cassis.

Combine the tequila and juices in a shaker with ice, and shake well. Strain into a martini glass. Gently pour in the crème de cassis so that it falls to the bottom, creating a layered effect.

1½ ounces **tequila**

¼ ounce freshly squeezed **orange juice**

¼ ounce freshly squeezed **lemon juice**

¼ ounce freshly squeezed **lime juice**

Dash of **crème de cassis**

Mezcal Sour

A sour can technically be made from any spirit, but some spirits work better than others. Good mezcal, like whiskey, is ideal for this drink because it can stand up to the sweet and sour components, with the unique, brassy, and slightly smoky taste of the spirit coming through.

Combine the mezcal, lemon juice, and sugar in a shaker with ice, and shake gently. Strain over a maraschino cherry in a martini glass.

1½ ounces **mezcal**

½ ounce freshly squeezed **lemon juice**

½ teaspoon **superfine sugar**

Maraschino cherry, for garnish

Brandy

Apple Sour*

French Connection

Pisco Canary*

Sidecar

*César original

When the art of distillation reached the wine-producing areas of Europe from the Middle East, winemakers knew a good thing when they saw it. Today almost every region of the world that makes wine also makes brandy. Some regions, such as Cognac and Armagnac, have eschewed wine altogether in favor of their eponymous spirits. The Spanish began making brandy more than a hundred years ago simply as a way to obtain spirits to fortify their sherry. Today, the Spanish are the world's biggest makers and consumers of brandy. Spanish brandy receives as much care and finesse as the sherry itself, and most of the brandies produced in Spain are aged in the same solera system as sherry.

Many drinkers overlook brandy at the bar. Just as sherry is often thought of as a rather staid beverage, brandy to some conjures images of all-male, postprandial musings in the library over cigars. Bartenders know, however, that brandy has a proud place at the bar and is an excellent cocktail ingredient. The Sidecar alone would secure its position in the bar rail. We encourage you to sample different brandies, from the elegant and refined Cognac to the sweeter, full-flavored labels from Spain. While you may not want to use two-hundred-dollar Napoleon brandy to mix cocktails, a good-quality spirit shouldn't be overlooked. Fortunately, many excellent but affordable labels from Spain, France, and California are available, all of which can make subtle but distinct variations in the drinks.

So, if you men out there are ever tempted to retreat to the library after dinner for brandy, for heaven's sake, take the women with you, and don't forget the lemons.

Apple Sour

1½ ounces **Calvados**

1 teaspoon **maple syrup**

¾ ounce freshly squeezed **lemon juice**

Maraschino cherry, for garnish

Most people don't think to stock maple syrup in the bar, but then most people don't think like us. Actually, when Dennis came up with this drink, he was surprised to find several references to maple syrup in the old bar books. The homey, rich flavor of the syrup makes for an inspired twist on the familiar Sidecar. Make sure to use only 100 percent pure maple syrup (but don't get confused and pour this drink on your morning pancakes).

Combine the Calvados, maple syrup, and lemon juice in a shaker with ice, and shake well, perhaps a little longer than usual to incorporate the syrup fully. Strain over a maraschino cherry in a martini glass.

French Connection

1 ounce **Cognac**

½ ounce **Grand Marnier**

Not all brandy should be enjoyed from a snifter—the fumes can become too intense, masking the subtleties of the spirit. However, this delightful after-dinner drink is one that works well in the traditional brandy glass. The inclusion of the orange liqueur adds a whole new dimension to the nose, allowing the aromas to meld into one harmonious and delicious experience. Vive la France!

Pour the Cognac and Grand Marnier into a brandy snifter and serve.

Pisco Canary

Pisco is Peruvian brandy, typically made from the moscato grape and aged in clay amphorae, as has been done since the Spaniards brought both the technique and the grapes to Peru. At César, we favor a type called Pisco Italia by La Botija, which has about it an almost eau-de-vie character, with a hint of pear. This is really a spin on a Pisco Sour, but frankly is much more delicious and interesting than the traditional version.

Combine the pisco, orange juice, and syrup in a shaker with ice, and shake well. Strain into a martini glass, and garnish with a slice of lime.

2 ounces **pisco**

½ ounce freshly squeezed **orange juice**

½ ounce **Lemon-Mint Simple Syrup** (page 17)

Lime slice, for garnish

Sidecar

Named for the bullet-shaped passenger cars attached to the sides of motorcycles—and allegedly after one gentleman in particular who frequented Harry's Bar in Paris after World War I—this is really a Brandy Sour. While the sweet and sour components can hide a multitude of sins, good brandy most assuredly enhances the drink. For a variation, try using a good Spanish brandy, which is often a tad sweeter and oakier than its French counterpart. Either way, try one to pique the appetite before dinner; and to continue the theme, finish with a little of the same brandy as a digestive.

Coat the rim of a martini glass with sugar. Combine the brandy, Cointreau, and lemon juice in a shaker with ice, and shake moderately. Strain into the glass, and garnish with a twist of lemon.

Superfine sugar, for coating rim of glass

1½ ounces **brandy**

½ ounce **Cointreau** or **triple sec**

¾ ounce freshly squeezed **lemon juice**

Twist of lemon, for garnish

Champagne

Bellini

César Champagne Cocktail*

César original

Why has Champagne always been the drink of choice for celebrations? The tiny bubbles have a lot to do with it; not only do they tickle the nose, but all that fizz causes the alcohol to enter the bloodstream much faster than other non-fizzy liquors. Good Champagne is also expensive, which some consider an endorphin release in itself.

Champagne comes from the region of the same name in the northeast corner of France, and has a relatively small annual production. It is made from basically two great grape varieties, chardonnay and pinot noir. When a label says *blanc de blanc,* it means it is made entirely from chardonnay, while *blanc de noir* indicates that pinot noir is the sole grape. What about all the rest of the bubbly stuff? Sorry, but if it's not from Champagne, made in the traditional manner prescribed by the laws of the region, it is simply sparkling wine, no matter how good it might be. That's a matter of nomenclature, however, and doesn't mean that other sparkling wines can't be fantastic. Cava from Spain; prosecco and a variety of spumanti from Italy; many great Champagne-style wines from the United States; and, of course, all the wonderful crémant wines from France (wines made outside of Champagne using the *méthode champenoise*) are all worthy sparklers.

There are other great reasons to love sparkling wines. Champagne is virtually calorie free, and no matter how well dressed one is, a champagne flute always looks better than a beer mug in your hand. While many people still amusingly think of Champagne as a drink for women, in our experience, men—while they may not ask for directions or drink pink drinks—will often gladly slam down cash for a bottle of the bubbly. At César, we pour a great deal of Champagne, Cava, and other sparkling wines, and they have also made their way into two of our favorite cocktails. The French 75, in the gin section, is another great Champagne cocktail.

Bellini

Forget the Mimosa. This is our version of the famous drink invented by Harry Cipriani at his bar in Venice. Harry's version calls exclusively for prosecco, the sparkling wine of the Veneto region, and is much simpler, relying on the quality of the sweet, local white peaches. Since most of us don't live in the near-perfect world of the Italian countryside, our addition of lemon juice and peach brandy intensifies the flavor of the peach puree. Using Champagne instead of prosecco makes for a richer, more full-bodied drink. We suggest you try both versions and choose your favorite.

Stir the peach puree, lemon juice, and brandy together in a champagne flute. Slowly fill with the sparkling wine of choice.

1 **white peach**, peeled, pitted, and pureed

2 dashes of freshly squeezed **lemon juice**

2 dashes of **peach brandy**

Chilled **prosecco** or **Champagne** to fill

César Champagne Cocktail

Our fortified version of the always elegant Champagne cocktail combines some of the products for which France is justly famous. The result is a dry, fruity, bubbly drink with many layers of flavor.

Pour the brandies into a champagne flute and fill with Champagne.

½ ounce **Armagnac**

½ ounce **Mandarine Napoleon brandy**

Chilled **Champagne** to fill

Coffee Drinks

Irish Coffee
Mandarin Coffee*
Mexican Coffee
*César original

Mexican Coffee

One doesn't have to wait for Saint Patrick's Day to enjoy an alcoholic coffee drink. These are great as nightcaps or to warm the soul on a rainy afternoon. We don't recommend them for breakfast, but then we're not your mother.

Irish Coffee

San Francisco is a long way from Tipperary, but in fact, that's where this delicious after-dinner drink-cum-Saint Patrick's Day staple gained its fame. Although Irish coffee is said to have been invented on the Emerald Isle, it's at the Buena Vista bar at Fisherman's Wharf in San Francisco that legions of Celtic wannabes have lined up for a little luck o' the Irish. The drink is really a takeoff on a traditional Irish "whiskey in tea," changed to coffee to appease traveling Americans. All the Irish whiskey consumed in this drink might partially make up for our almost ruining Ireland's whiskey industry during Prohibition. (Before Prohibition, the United States was Ireland's biggest customer.) Erin go bragh!

1½ ounces **Irish whiskey**

Dash of **Cointreau**

Sugar cube (optional)

Strong, hot, black **coffee** to fill

1 teaspoon **heavy cream**

Whipped cream, for topping

Pour the whiskey and Cointreau into a heat-resistant glass mug. For those who like their coffee sweet, place a sugar cube in the mug. Add the coffee, stir to blend, and slowly pour in the cream. Top with a dollop of whipped cream.

Mandarin Coffee

1 ounce **Mandarine Napoleon brandy**

1 ounce **Baileys Irish Cream**

½ ounce **Kahlúa**

Strong, hot, black **coffee** to fill

Whipped cream, for topping

The flavors of orange, chocolate, coffee, and cream meld together to form a soothing, exotic, and delicious hot drink.

Combine the brandy, Baileys, and Kahlúa in a heat-resistant glass mug. Fill with coffee, stir to blend, and top with a dollop of whipped cream.

Mexican Coffee

1 ounce **tequila**

1 ounce **Kahlúa**

Strong, hot, black **coffee** to fill

Whipped cream, for topping

With the rich, coffee-chocolate flavor of the Kahlúa, this is more of a dessert than an after-dinner drink—a dessert with a kick. You don't have to wait until after dinner, though; Mexican coffee is a great comforter for a rainy afternoon, or a cold winter's night.

Combine the tequila and Kahlúa in a heat-resistant glass mug. Fill with coffee, stir to blend, and top with a dollop of whipped cream.

Wine

Dennis Lapuyade is one of the partners in César, and he selects and buys all the wines and spirits. Tall and dapper, and easily the most serious and erudite member of the family, his encyclopedic knowledge of wine, grapes, and winemaking continually astounds us. With his many years of experience in the wine business, coupled with his personal interest in the subject, we thought who better to talk about our eclectic selection of wines and spirits?

∞∞

While the wine list at César features bottles from around the world, the offerings from Spain intrigue us the most.

Spain is the third largest producer of table wine in the world, trailing only Italy and France in annual production. Interestingly, Spain's annual production almost doubled in the decade between 1988 and 1998, while France and Italy both showed significant annual declines. Even so, Spain has one of the lowest average yields per hectare (2.47 acres), at 26 hectoliters; Italy comes in at a whopping 60 hectoliters per hectare, and

France at a substantial 58. (Smaller yields typically produce superior wines since all of nature's wiles can be focused on fewer grapes, thus intensifying the sugars.) This phenomenon is attributable to the greater age of the Spanish vineyards and the lack of significant new plantings in the decade of the 1990s. Look for the average yield to climb as new plantings and youthful vigor take hold.

Whatever the statistics and numbers reveal, they tell only part of the story about the current revolution in Spanish winemaking. Substantial foreign investment is taking place in all areas of Spain, including Rioja, Ribera del Duero and environs (including Sardon del Duero), Toro, Catalonia (including Costers del Segre), Penedès, Tarragona, Conca de Barberà, and, most notably, the Priorat. Not to be outdone by foreigners, many local wineries, including the venerable Cava house Segura Viudas, have purchased far-flung properties in La Ribera, the Priorat, and Rías Baixas. Old, traditional bodegas all over Spain are investing in new infrastructure and ideas. The young guard, led by Alvaro Palacios, has ventured forth to help resurrect abandoned vineyards in the Priorat, Bierzo,

Does the season or the food on the menu influence your wine selections?
Absolutely. And in thinking about the menu, we have found that European wines have a particular affinity for the food at the restaurant. These wines tend to be more subtle and less fruity and alcoholic than domestic wines. The delicateness of the European wines complements the food without overpowering it, creating a beautiful symbiosis with the tapas.

How do you effectively taste and compare the wines to others that you have tasted before?
I have been tasting and enjoying wines for over thirty-five years. Through my own personal consumption, and in looking for wines for César, I have developed a taste memory that helps me to compare the wines with all of the other wines that I have tasted to date. The palate is like a muscle that needs consistent exercise and attention, and it is only through regular tastings that a comprehensive taste memory is established and maintained. When I speak of bringing something to the wine, I am talking about my taste memory. By comparing my collective experiences and noted characteristics of a certain varietal, I am able to pick up on new or subtle variations in the wine.

A Note About Pairing Wine and Food

The very idea of struggling to find the right wine for the right food is a completely modern concept, and one that is fraught with misconceptions, generalities, and outdated rules. Familiar guidelines such as "red wine with meat, white wine with fish" might seem foolproof until one considers a big, oaky California chardonnay with a delicate piece of white fish. And what about salmon? Surely it can stand up to lighter-bodied reds, and no doubt fare better than with an ethereal white wine. And is a full-bodied white wine paired with pork wrong?

The agonizing that many Americans go through when matching wine and food is amusing to our European cousins, who for eons have washed down their regional dishes with the local quaff. And guess what? It's usually a great match. Throughout winemaking history, the wine and food of a particular region have been inseparable and, indeed, have grown out of the same soil (what grows together, goes together). We have no such legacy here in the New World. In fact, after Prohibition, the Great Depression, and World War II—the 1-2-3 knockout punch for wine consumption in America—followed by the white-bread years of the Eisenhower administration, it's a wonder that we drink wine at all. Unfortunate also is that in relearning how to eat and drink, we have let the wine snobs do all the talking. Our hopeless obsession with quantifying everything has led to a reliance on wine ratings that have nothing to do with food, instead of trusting our own ability to taste and discern what we like.

This is not to say that a little knowledge isn't a good thing, nor that there aren't some terrific matches out there that have stood the test of time. Roast lamb and Cabernet Sauvignon comes to mind, or foie gras and Sauternes. But just as most of us believe that the best wines are the wines we like best, there are food and wine pairings that for one person are a match made in heaven and to another are the equivalent of culinary hell. A crisp, steely, high-acid white wine may seem the perfect foil for raw oysters, but who's to say that those same little bivalves might not be equally glorious with a dry Martini?

Adding to this conundrum is the tapas menu, the very nature of which invites one to try a variety of dishes, from seafood to meat to vegetables. How, then, to make the perfect wine and food match? One must first accept that there is no perfect food and wine match, although certainly some are better than others. We don't offer wine pairing suggestions on the menu at César because most orders consist of such a variety of dishes. Instead, all of our wines are chosen for their ability to go with food. We always offer a varied selection of wines by the glass, as well as our vast offerings of sherries, spirits, cocktails, and beer, all of which can be the perfect accompaniment to a variety of tapas. Finding the right match for you should be a personal discovery guided by what works for you and enhances your experience, not someone else's idea of what the "correct" pairing should be. So relax and have a Sidecar with those fried potatoes.

Tapas

Bar-hopping has a different meaning in Spain than it does here in America. In Spain, one is not so much in search of more drinks, although there are plenty of those in the form of sherry, wine, and beer. Rather, the *tapeo,* or tapas bar–hopping, a centuries-old ritual that continues unabated all across Spain, is as much about food and social interaction as it is about libations. Every day at lunchtime and in the early evening after work, the tapas bars are full of people, young and old, who are gathered, mostly standing, to have a nibble or a whole meal and to converse with friends or colleagues about the day's events, last night's soccer scores, or the latest government fiasco.

Traditionally, tapas were a prelude to a main meal later in the evening, similar to appetizers. Today, however, they are as likely to constitute the meal itself, especially at lunchtime. These little dishes may seem small, but when several are consumed with friends, they can be very satisfying indeed. It is not uncommon for friends to visit several bars over the course of the evening, having a drink and a tapa in each place and moving on to the next.

There are several theories as to the origin of this ritual, but the most plausible and most accepted is that tapas began in sherry country, in and around Jerez de la Frontera. *Tapa* means "cover" or "lid," derived from the verb *tapar,* meaning to "cover up." In the hot, dusty Andalusian countryside, as caballeros sat drinking their afternoon sherry, something would be placed atop the *copita,* or sherry glass, to keep out the flies and dust. Originally, this might have been a small plate or even a piece of bread, on which eventually the savvy innkeepers added a piece of ham or cheese or a few olives, and thus a singular national tradition was born.

Tapas can be almost anything, from a slice of the region's great air-cured ham to elaborately prepared dishes involving seafood or meat. In other words, the tradition has more to do with how the food is served than with what is actually on the plate. However, many now-classic tapas appear on menus throughout Spain, while others appear regionally, based on local raw materials or customs. The selection of tapas we present here is a good overview of the range of delicacies one might encounter traveling in Spain, and yet they are not necessarily meant to be definitive versions. Our recipes were developed by our chef, Maggie Pond, as well as by the original chef, David Tanis, but they are all inspired by, and respectful of, the ingredients and traditions of Spanish tapas bars.

∞·∞

César chef Maggie Pond was introduced to Spanish cuisine at her first cooking job out of college. Although one of the restaurant owners was Spanish, Maggie realizes looking back that the food was far from authentic. Even so, her interest in Spanish food was piqued and she gained familiarity with many of the ingredients for which Spain is known. She continued to work in non-Spanish establishments such as the late Barbara Tropp's seminal restaurant, China Moon, in San Francisco, and the prestigious BayWolf in Oakland. At the latter, she worked through weekly regional menus where they "hit Spain every few weeks," adding to her knowledge and enthusiasm for the cuisine. She knew, however, that ultimately she had to go to the source. Cookbook author Miramar Torres, scion of the famous Spanish winemaking family, arranged for Maggie to go to Spain and work. This and subsequent trips to Spain fueled her interest in Spanish cooking, and tapas in particular, a passion that eventually landed her in a class back in the States taught by David Tanis, one of the original chefs at Chez Panisse and an aficionado of Spanish and Latin cuisine, who had recently been hired to devise the menu for César. David, in turn, hired Maggie, who has been at the helm ever since. "David taught me to think of César as a great sushi bar," remembers Maggie. "Tapas are simple, so the ingredients have to be the finest and freshest. It also happens to be a great time for Spanish products in this country, products such as *piquillo* peppers, *jamón serrano*, olive oils, and all that excellent seafood." Maggie prefers to stay as authentic as possible in terms of the ingredients and cooking styles, and she goes to Spain at least once a year to cook and eat in order to keep the well from going dry. She will, however, mix regional specialties, combining such things as *piquillo* peppers (from Navarre in the north) with *mojo verde* (a favorite sauce from the Canary Islands).

Tapas just might be Spain's greatest culinary legacy to the world. More and more of today's diners prefer to compose their meal from the appetizer menu, which is basically what a tapas bar is all about. Doing so allows you to taste a range of foods, never tiring of any one dish. It also enables you to order as much or as little as you want. Having tapas with a group encourages camaraderie and social interaction. Tapas also underscore the Spanish and European custom of always having food with drink. It is almost impossible in Spain to order an alcoholic beverage without some form of food accompanying it, even if it is a basket of bread or some cured olives. The wisdom of this is obvious, and it is unusual to see drunks staggering out of a tapas bar.

We hope you will try a selection of our tapas, either for yourself or for a party. As evidenced by the scene at César just about every night, tapas are the ideal party food. Many of our recipes, such as the Croquetas de Arroz con Jamón y Yerbas, Empanadillas with Pork Filling and Pimentón Dough, Cumin Fried Chicken with Watercress and Blood Orange Alioli, and all the potato dishes, to name but a few, can be made easily in large quantities and are proven crowd pleasers. Many of our salads and vegetable dishes make wonderfully simple dinners, whether served as tapas or not, and in fact, any of these recipes could be served as a big meal rather than a little one. We hope you enjoy them, and if you are ever in Berkeley, we hope you will stop in for a drink and a tapa or two.

The Tapas Pantry

Spain produces a legendary array of products for the pantry, and we use many of them at César. The Spanish were among the first Europeans to implement a Denomination of Origin (DO) classification for certain food products, similar to and inspired by the DO system for wines. Products that garner this prestigious certification must adhere to strict guidelines according to the type of food. Many of these food products that were virtually unobtainable a decade ago in the United States are now widely available in supermarkets, specialty stores, and by mail order (see Resources). While there are possible substitutions for some of these items, we urge you to seek out the authentic Spanish goods whenever you can in order to capture the true taste of Spain.

Boquerones (Anchovies)

If there is anything more ubiquitous than ham in Spanish tapas bars, it is the luscious little hand-filleted, hand-packed *boquerones,* or anchovies. Gleaned from the icy Atlantic waters off the north coast of Cantabria, these are unlike any anchovies you've ever had. Noticeably missing is the intense saltiness of most commercial anchovies and the unpleasant fishiness that usually overwhelms the palate, bringing in cries of "hold the anchovies." *Boquerones* are white, slightly tart, and are almost always packed in one of two ways—either in olive oil or in a combination of oil and vinegar, resulting in delicate fish that is pickled or, more accurately, *en escabèche,* as the Spanish say. They typically come packaged in refrigerated plastic containers that render them as fresh and tasty as if you were eating them in San Sebastián. They work well as ingredients or can be eaten right out of the container.

Capers and Caperberries

The caper bush, *Capparis spinosa,* has always grown wild in Spain and was highly regarded by the Romans and subsequently by the Moors, both of whom helped firmly establish these flavorful little buds in Spanish cuisine. Capers are actually the unopened buds of the bush, picked before they have a chance to flower. When they have already blossomed, they are left to mature further into caperberries, the real fruit of the plant. Typically, capers are immediately put up in brine to halt their growth, and then they are left to ferment. However, some capers are dried and packed in sea salt, which actually better preserves the natural, floral taste of the buds. Maggie uses only salt-packed capers at César because they have more flavor. They are not as readily available as brined capers but can be easily purchased by mail order. To use salt-packed capers, simply rinse them lightly. Brined capers, especially when rinsed, are really more about texture, with much of the flavor left behind in the brine. Caperberries are used for garnish at César. With their long stem still attached, they are more like olives and are a fine accompaniment to a wide variety of tapas.

Chiles, Peppers, and Pimentón

Columbus, in his search for *Piper nigrum*, or black pepper, forever screwed up the nomenclature for the countless pungent pods of the *Capsicum* genus, all of which can trace their roots to Latin America. Semantics aside, several types of peppers in several different forms have become an important part of Spanish cuisine.

Ñora chiles. These squat, bell-shaped chiles are sold dried and are most commonly used as a flavoring for *romesco* sauce. They must be reconstituted before using. If you can't find them, dried *cascabels* are a good substitute.

Piquillo peppers. There are roasted red peppers, and then there are *piquillos*. These small peppers, sold in jars, are grown in Navarre in the north of Spain and are so distinctive that they have been given the prestigious DO. They are about an inch across the top, no more than two or three inches long, and intensely red. They are always hand-picked, roasted over an open beechwood fire, and hand-peeled to preserve the flavor (no water is ever used). Slightly spicy and wildly delicious, *piquillos* can be eaten out of the jar or incorporated into an array of beguiling tapas. They are perfect for stuffing with cheese, seafood, or vegetables and are one of the true glories of the Spanish pantry.

Pimentón. This is the paprika of Spain. It is made of dried, ground pimiento peppers and can be sweet or hot, and smoked or not. The most famous *pimentón* comes from northern Extremadura and the valley of La Vera, one of the first places in Europe to receive and experiment with the new peppers. *Pimentón de la Vera* comes in mild *(dulce)*, medium hot *(agridulce)*, and hot *(picante)* versions. The peppers are smoked for several days over oak fires, resulting in one of the most distinctive flavors found in Spanish food. The *pimentón* from Murcia in the southeast is traditionally dried in the sun or in drying chambers but is not smoked. It is used extensively in the production of chorizo.

Jamón Serrano

Like many great foods from around the world, *jamón serrano* (literally, "mountain ham") was originally developed to preserve a staple—in this case, pork—for the lean winter months. However, over time it has become one of the most highly regarded products in the gastronomical world. It is unfair to call these hams raw; rather, they are uncooked. The method of production is similar to that of its famous Italian cousin, *prosciutto di Parma*. First the hind leg of the pig is cleaned and salted and left in the salt for several days or weeks. The salt has a double effect of drawing out moisture while inhibiting the growth of harmful bacteria. After a specific amount of time, typically the number of days equal to the weight of the ham, the hams are hung to air-cure for a year or more in lofts through which the pristine mountain breezes circulate, slowly transforming the meat into buttery, supple hams.

Jamón serrano is a wonderfully versatile ham, delicious on its own, sliced thin and laid out on a plate, or used as an ingredient in salads, sandwiches, pizzas, and pastas. Currently there are two producers in Spain who have garnered United States Department of Agriculture approval to export to the United States—Redondo Iglesias and Navidul—with rumors that a third is close to getting the okay. Many delis and gourmet shops that carry prosciutto now also have Spanish hams. You can substitute Italian prosciutto if you can't get hold of *jamón serrano*.

Olive Oil

Olive oil lies at the heart of the cooking in Spain and certainly at César. Maggie uses two types of olive oil for her basic cooking and finishing needs, one from Spain and one from Italy. Stephen Singer, a noted wine authority and one of the partners in César, imports several extra virgin olive oils from Tuscany's Chianti region. His signature oil, Stephen Singer Olio Extra Vergine (see Resources), is a favorite of Maggie's, and she uses it anytime she wants the flavor of the olives to shine through, such as for finishing a cooked dish or drizzling over *jamón serrano*. Not as aggressive as most Tuscan oils, this is a softer, almost buttery version with bright, fruity flavors. Like all of Stephen's oils, it is unfiltered to retain as much flavor, perfume, and overall characteristics as possible.

For all-purpose cooking and sautéing, Maggie uses a Spanish extra virgin olive oil from a cooperative in Catalonia called Unio. Made primarily from arbequina olives, this is a lovely, straightforward oil that enhances any cooked food. Whichever type of olive oil you use, make sure it is extra virgin, meaning that it contains less than 1 percent acidity.

Saffron

The world's most expensive spice, saffron is the hand-picked and lightly toasted threads from the stigma of a type of crocus *(Crocus sativus)* harvested throughout La Mancha each October. Although saffron *(azafrán* in Spanish, from the Arabic *az-zafaran,* meaning "yellow") is native to Asia Minor, the saffron from Spain is generally regarded as the best. Make sure you buy saffron in whole threads and not powder. The powdered form may not be true saffron, and even if it is, it has probably lost all its flavor and aroma in the grinding. Don't be too alarmed at the price of saffron; a little goes a long way.

Salt

Throughout the recipes in this book, salt always means kosher salt or sea salt. Kosher salt is a good, all-purpose salt for the kitchen. The larger grains make it easy to pinch with your fingers and to keep track of how much you are using, and it contains no added chemicals. Technically, all salt is sea salt—salt deposits are the result of prehistoric oceans that once covered most of the earth. Sea salt is generally preferred by chefs and comes in many degrees of coarseness and flavor. Due to the size of its grains, regular table salt is about twice as salty by volume as either kosher salt or sea salt, so if you use it, you will need to reduce the measurements by about half.

Vinegar

Vinegar is the ultimate result of the winemaking process and is a valued cooking ingredient in any great wine-producing country. At César, we use both red wine vinegar and sherry vinegar. Red wine vinegar is made by introducing aceto bacteria into wine and allowing it to consume the alcohol and turn it into acid. Good vinegar is aged in wood barrels for several months to allow it to mellow and take on flavors from the oak.

Sherry vinegar is made in much the same way as sherry itself (see pages 8–9), and like the sherry process, it sort of decides its own fate. In the sherry bodegas, the winemakers know when a barrel is not going to turn out and is headed down the path toward becoming vinegar. It is sent to a separate bodega, where it will pass through a similar solera system, or a continual blending of the old and the new in stacks of barrels. When vinegar is taken from the bottom barrel for bottling, the barrel (which is never emptied) is replenished from the barrel directly above. That one in turn is topped off from the barrel above it, and so on. Finally, the top row of barrels is refilled with freshly inoculated sherry. Sherry vinegars can be aged for many years, and the best take on depths of flavor rich with the essence of toasted nuts and the wood in which it matured.

Soups

One doesn't always consider tapas and soup in the same context. With tapas, one thinks of quick bites to accompany a drink, oftentimes standing up. Soups are meant to be savored, with the diner blowing on each spoonful and dipping bread in the bowl. That said, we couldn't resist including our versions of these classic soups from Spain that are always popular at César.

In the early 1980s, chef Felipe Rojas-Lombardi opened what was surely the first authentic tapas bar in the United States, the Ballroom in New York City. A curious blend of tapas bar and cabaret, Felipe's place served these strange new "little dishes" to New York sophisticates. One of his signature items was what he called soup tapas, or three different creamy soups served in espresso cups. It was just enough of each soup to enjoy as a prelude to the rest of the tapas that were to come. It is in this spirit that we include soups in our tapas book.

Gazpacho

English Cucumber Gazpacho with Piquillo Pepper Relish

Caldo Gallego

Gazpacho

SERVES 6

Roasted Tomatoes

10 to 12 ripe **tomatoes**, cut into wedges

½ cup **extra virgin olive oil**

Salt and freshly ground **black pepper**

Soup

1½ cups **ice water**

2 tablespoons **sherry vinegar**

1 cup cubed day-old **bread**

½ cup **piquillo peppers** (see page 87), coarsely chopped, plus ¾ cup finely diced

¾ cup peeled, seeded, and coarsely chopped **English cucumbe**r, plus ¾ cup finely diced (about 1 cucumber total)

1 clove **garlic** (more if desired)

1½ teaspoons **salt**

¼ cup **extra virgin olive oil**

Garnish

1 small **red onion**, finely diced

Finely chopped fresh **flat-leaf parsley**

Fried Croutons (page 202)

Extra virgin olive oil

Freshly squeezed **lemon juice**

Many Americans have the idea that everyone in Spain, looking rather like Carmen or Don Juan, eats nothing but cool, tomatoey gazpacho all day and paella at night. Many of these same Americans would be surprised to learn that the first recipes for gazpacho didn't even contain tomatoes (remember, Europeans didn't know about tomatoes until well into the sixteenth century), and many still don't. The basic ingredients, eaten since Roman times, are garlic, bread, vinegar, olive oil, and water, with various vegetables added later. To the shepherds in the austere hills of Andalusia, this soup, which translates roughly to "leftovers," was intended as sustenance and a means of quenching thirst.

At César, we have developed several versions of this classic vegetable soup, each deliciously cold and satisfying. Roasting the tomatoes first may seem like a lot of extra work, but the deep tomato flavor and richer texture make the step worthwhile. Most cooks agree that gazpacho is best made in a high-speed blender, but you can also use a food processor.

To roast the tomatoes, preheat the oven to 375°F. Line a baking sheet with parchment paper. Toss the tomatoes with the olive oil in a large bowl and season with salt and pepper. Spread them out evenly, skin side down, on the baking sheet. Roast until they release their juices and begin to caramelize on the edges, 30 to 40 minutes. You should have about 2½ cups.

To make the soup, combine the water and vinegar in a medium bowl, add the bread, and soak for a few minutes. In a blender, combine the roasted tomatoes, soaked bread and liquid, the coarsely chopped *piquillos* and cucumber, garlic, and salt, and purée. With the blender running, slowly add the oil. Taste and adjust the seasoning. Remove the soup from the blender and stir in the diced cucumbers and *piquillos*. Cover and chill for at least 1 hour.

To serve, top each portion with red onion, parsley, croutons, a drizzle of oil, and a drop of lemon juice, or place the garnishes on the table in small dishes and let diners add their own.

English Cucumber Gazpacho
with Piquillo Pepper Relish

SERVES 8

Relish

½ cup **piquillo peppers** (see page 87), finely diced

2 tablespoons minced **fresh mint** or **basil**, or a combination

2 tablespoons **extra virgin olive oil**

2 teaspoons **red wine vinegar**

Salt and freshly ground **black pepper**

Soup

8 cups peeled, seeded, and coarsely chopped **English cucumbers** (about 4 cucumbers total)

1¼ cups **extra virgin olive oil**

1 cup **ice water**

1 clove **garlic**

½ cup **white wine vinegar**

2 tablespoons freshly squeezed **lemon juice**

2 teaspoons **salt**

¼ teaspoon freshly ground **black pepper**

½ teaspoon **cayenne pepper**

Fried Croutons (page 202), for garnish

Extra virgin olive oil, for drizzling

This version of our gazpacho harks back to the soup's humble origins in that it contains no tomato. Instead, cucumber takes center stage. It is one of the most refreshing soups you can imagine for the dog days of summer, or for when you're dreaming of the dog days of summer. A high-speed blender produces the best results, although a food processor can be used.

To make the relish, combine the peppers, mint, oil, and vinegar in a small bowl and season to taste with salt and pepper. Let stand for at least a half hour before using.

To make the soup, place half each of the cucumbers, oil, water, garlic, vinegar, lemon juice, salt, pepper, and cayenne in a blender and purée. Pour into a serving bowl and repeat with the rest of the soup ingredients. Cover and chill for at least 1 hour before serving. (The soup can be made up to 1 day in advance.)

To serve, top each portion with croutons, a spoonful of relish, and a drizzle of extra virgin olive oil.

Caldo Gallego

Gallego *refers to someone or something from Galicia, the lush, verdant region in northwest Spain, directly north of Portugal, while* caldo *means "broth." If you ate this dish in five different restaurants or homes, you would invariably enjoy five different versions. Beans, pork in some form, and greens are the basics that everyone agrees on, but beyond that it depends on what is in season and what is in the garden. Our version evolved from having to make it to order, or* à la minute, *as the French say. Therefore all the components are cooked separately and combined at the end in the pork broth. This also means that everything can be cooked ahead of time for entertaining at home, and put together at the last minute.*

Soak the beans overnight in fresh, cold water.

The next day, place the potatoes in a saucepan with salted water to cover and bring to a rapid boil. Cover immediately with a tight-fitting lid, remove from the heat, and let the potatoes finish cooking in the residual heat until you can easily pierce them with a paring knife, about 1 hour. Drain and let cool.

While the potatoes are cooking, drain the beans. Wrap the thyme, garlic, bay leaf, peppercorns, carrot, and onion in cheesecloth, and tie with a string. Combine the beans and the aromatics in a large pot, cover with water, and bring to a boil. Turn down the heat and simmer until tender, 30 to 45 minutes. Salt the beans to taste about halfway through the cooking time. Remove the cheesecloth sack and discard. Drain the beans and set aside.

Meanwhile, blanch the chard in salted water for 5 minutes. Drain.

Cut the potatoes into eighths and add them to a large pot with the beans, chard, stock, and sausage. Bring to a simmer over medium-high heat and cook until all the ingredients are heated through, about 10 minutes. Ladle into bowls and top with the parsley.

SERVES 8

2 cups **white beans**, such as navy or cannellini beans

8 **new potatoes**

½ bunch **thyme**

5 cloves **garlic**

1 **bay leaf**

1 teaspoon **black peppercorns**

1 large **carrot**, peeled and coarsely chopped

1 **yellow onion**, coarsely chopped

Salt

1 head **red chard**, stems removed and leaves coarsely chopped

4 cups **Roasted Pork Stock** (page 202)

4 cooked **pork or garlic sausages**, cut into ¼-inch slices

Chopped fresh **flat-leaf parsley**, for garnish

Salads & Vegetables

Salads and vegetable tapas make up the majority of our menu on most days at César. We are blessed here in California with a bounty of great produce throughout the year, and we try to take advantage of that whenever we can. The recipes, however, can be put together without any exotic vegetables, at least no more exotic than an artichoke. The only dish that may give you trouble is the Fried Pimientos de Padrón; check out the Resources for possible suppliers of these delicious and unique peppers.

Most of these dishes are stand-alone salads, but the quartet of grilled and roasted vegetables, starting with the Roasted Artichokes, are best served together. Just arrange the vegetables on a platter with an accompanying bowl of *romesco* sauce and let everyone dig in. The serving sizes are tapas portions, but any of the recipes could easily be doubled for an entrée. The Smoked Trout and Persimmon Salad or the Poached Salmon are particularly satisfying main-course salads.

Smoked Trout and Persimmon Salad with Creamy Sherry Vinaigrette

Fried Pimientos de Padrón

Spinach Tortilla

Chicken Escabèche Salad with Piquillo Peppers

Romaine Salad with Valdéon

Roasted Artichokes with Romesco

Roasted New Potatoes with Romesco

Roasted Eggplant with Romesco

Grilled Spring Onions with Romesco

Escarole Salad

Mushrooms al Ajillo

Beet Salad with Anise Seed Vinaigrette

Poached Salmon with Cilantro and Cumin Vinaigrette

Smoked Trout and Persimmon Salad
with Creamy Sherry Vinaigrette

Smoked trout lends itself to salads because of its flaky, nonoily texture, and it marries perfectly with persimmons. Be sure to use the Fuyu variety of persimmon, the kind that can be eaten out of hand. (What are sold as persimmons here are actually kaki fruit, a relative of the persimmon; but grown in California they have come to be regarded as persimmons, and who are we to argue, especially over such a tasty salad?)

Cut off the main stems of the watercress, usually right above the twist tie. Allow the cress to fall apart, breaking it apart slightly; the idea is to keep it in little sections or florets. Cut off the base of each endive and cut the rest on the diagonal into ½-inch slices.

Place the greens and persimmons in a large bowl and season with salt and pepper. Break apart the trout gently, keeping it in medium-sized pieces, and set aside.

To make the vinaigrette, combine the shallot, vinegar, salt, pepper, and sugar in a medium bowl and let stand for 20 minutes. In a food processor, combine the vinegar mixture and the egg and blend for 30 seconds. With the machine running, slowly pour in the oil until the mixture emulsifies, then add the water.

Toss the salad with enough vinaigrette to coat it evenly without saturating it. Divide among individual plates. Place the trout in the bowl and coat with the remaining dressing. Divide the trout among the salads, arranging it on top.

SERVES 8

1 bunch **watercress**

4 heads **Belgian endive**

2 **Fuyu persimmons**, peeled, quartered, and sliced crosswise

Salt and freshly ground **black pepper**

1 pound **smoked trout fillets**, skin removed

Vinaigrette

1 **shallot**, finely diced

3 tablespoons **sherry vinegar**

1 teaspoon **salt**

½ teaspoon freshly ground **black pepper**

1 teaspoon **sugar**

1 **egg**

1 cup **extra virgin olive oil**

1 teaspoon **water**

Fried Pimientos de Padrón

SERVES 6

1 cup **extra virgin olive oil**

1 pound **Padrón peppers**

1 tablespoon **salt**

Chiles originated in South America, and were among the first foods taken back to Europe from the New World. Cultures throughout Latin America fry up batches of chiles that are eaten as snacks or incorporated into other dishes. The pungent little pods in this recipe are named for a small town in Galicia, where they provide the livelihood for a couple of hundred families. Aside from accompanying the local meat dishes, the peppers are served in tapas bars throughout the country. Our stock is grown locally, in East Palo Alto at Happy Quail Farm. Owner David Winsberg was already cultivating a variety of peppers when a friend introduced him to the singular Padrón. They are essentially baby peppers, and the earlier they are picked, the milder they are. However, even when they are mild, there can be plenty of hot ones in any given batch, and that is one of the wonderfully enigmatic things about chiles. As the Galicians say, algunas pican, y otros no, *or "some are hot and some are not."*

Heat the oil to 375°F in a heavy-bottomed pan or a cast-iron skillet. Drop in a handful of peppers at a time and, using a slotted spoon, keep turning them until their skins begin to blister and turn lightly brown, 2 to 3 minutes. Remove them from the oil and toss in a bowl with some of the salt. Repeat with the remaining chiles. Serve immediately.

Spinach Tortilla

SERVES 8

1½ pounds **spinach**, tough stems removed and rinsed

¼ cup **dried currants**

½ cup **pine nuts**

½ cup **extra virgin olive oil**

2 y**ellow onions**, thinly sliced

1 tablespoon finely chopped **garlic**

⅛ teaspoon ground **nutmeg**

⅛ teaspoon **cayenne pepper**

½ teaspoon **salt**

7 **eggs**

Freshly ground **black pepper**

Pickled red onions, for garnish

How the Mexican tortilla got its name is something of a mystery, since the only thing it has in common with the Spanish original is its shape. Unlike the Mexican flatbread made of either corn or wheat, a tortilla (literally "little cake") in Spain is a round, relatively flat omelet, or what the Italians call a frittata. They are ubiquitous in tapas bars throughout the country. There are two ways to cook a tortilla, both requiring a little practice. The first is to cook the eggs halfway and then invert the omelet and slide it back into the pan to finish cooking. In Spain, they actually use a ceramic disk with a handle designed specifically for flipping tortillas, but you can use a relatively flat plate or pot lid as long as it's bigger in diameter than the pan. Another method is to use a cast-iron pan and, after the initial cooking stage, slip the whole pan under the broiler to finish. It's easier than trying to flip the tortilla, and it produces a wonderfully golden brown top. Whichever method you choose, this is a terrific dish in which to use up leftovers since almost anything can go into it, such as cooked vegetables and potatoes, roasted peppers, mushrooms, bits of ham, and even pasta. Our version can make a meal unto itself, accompanied by a salad and a glass of wine.

Blanch the spinach by plunging it into boiling salted water for about 30 seconds. Remove and drain. When the spinach is cool enough to handle, squeeze out the excess water and chop coarsely.

Put the currants in a small bowl of warm water, let soak for 15 minutes, and then drain. Meanwhile, toast the pine nuts in a dry skillet (preferably cast-iron) over medium heat, stirring frequently, until golden brown, about 7 minutes.

Heat ¼ cup of the oil in a skillet over medium heat, and slowly caramelize the onions, cooking them until they take on a deep amber color, about 30 minutes. Add the garlic and cook for another 5 minutes. Remove from the heat and drain off the oil.

In a large bowl, mix the onions and garlic with the spinach, currants, pine nuts, nutmeg, cayenne, and salt. In another large bowl, whisk the eggs and season with salt and black pepper. Fold in the spinach mixture.

Heat the remaining ¼ cup oil in a 10-inch nonstick skillet over medium heat. Pour in the spinach-egg mixture and scramble lightly. Turn down the heat to medium-low and cook until the tortilla has begun to form a bottom crust, about 5 minutes. Using a plate or a pot lid, invert the tortilla, slide it back into the pan, tucking in the edge to form the shape, and continue to cook until it feels firm to the touch, 3 to 4 minutes. Cut into wedges and garnish with pickled red onions.

Chicken Escabèche Salad
with Piquillo Peppers

SERVES 8

6 **chicken thighs**
(about 4 ounces each)

Salt and freshly ground **black pepper**

¼ cup **extra virgin olive oil**

Marinade

1 cup **Roasted Chicken Stock**
(page 202)

2 **yellow onions**, thinly sliced

6 tablespoons thinly sliced **garlic**

1 cup **sherry vinegar**

½ teaspoon crumbled **saffron
threads**

1 tablespoon **salt**

3 **bay leaves**

10 **black peppercorns**

2 sprigs **rosemary**

2 sprigs **thyme**

10 **red new potatoes**

1 cup **extra virgin olive oil**

Salt and freshly ground **black pepper**

2 cups **piquillo peppers** (see page 87),
cut into ¼-inch julienne

2 cups loosely packed **arugula leaves**

One normally thinks of an escabèche *as being made with seafood or fish. However, this wonderful pickling method also works well for this chicken salad. Maggie prefers thigh meat because it is a little fattier and more flavorful than breast meat. The method for cooking the potatoes allows them to cook thoroughly without the skins bursting open. To cure the chicken properly, it should be prepared a day in advance.*

To prepare the chicken, preheat the oven to 375°F. Salt, pepper, and oil the chicken thighs. Place on a rack in a roasting pan, and roast for 45 minutes. Transfer the cooked chicken to a wide, shallow baking dish and set aside.

Meanwhile, prepare the marinade by combining the stock, onions, garlic, vinegar, saffron, and salt in a medium nonreactive saucepan. Tie the bay leaves, peppercorns, rosemary, and thyme in cheesecloth and add to the saucepan. Bring the mixture to a boil, then turn the heat down to a slow simmer and cook for 10 minutes. Remove the cheesecloth bundle and discard. Pour the marinade over the chicken, cover, and refrigerate overnight.

To cook the potatoes, place them in a large saucepan with salted water to cover and bring to a rapid boil. Cover immediately with a tight-fitting lid, remove from the heat, and let the potatoes finish cooking in the residual heat until you can easily pierce them with a paring knife, about 1 hour. Drain and let cool. Cut the potatoes into quarters.

Preheat the oven to 375°F. Line a sheet pan with parchment paper. Toss the potatoes in a large bowl with ½ cup of the oil and season with salt and pepper. Spread them skin side down on the sheet pan and roast until they are crisp on the outside and have a golden, roasted color, about 15 minutes. Let cool to room temperature.

Take the chicken out of the marinade and remove and discard the skin. Pull the meat from the bones, tearing it into bite-sized pieces, and return the pieces to the marinade. Stir in the remaining ½ cup oil and the peppers.

Just before serving, put the potatoes and arugula in a large bowl. Stir up the chicken and marinade and, using a slotted spoon, transfer the mixture to the bowl, leaving behind most of the liquid in the marinade. Toss everything together and serve immediately.

Romaine Salad
with Valdeón

This salad features a Spanish take on a blue cheese dressing. Be careful not to chop the shallots for the vinaigrette too finely, as they act as another vegetable in the salad. Valdeón is a creamy, handcrafted cow's milk blue cheese from the valley of Valdeón in León, at the southern end of the Picos de Europa mountain range. A close cousin to the more assertive Cabrales from the northern side of the mountains, Valdeón is wrapped in chestnut leaves and allowed to mature in the ancient caves of the region. Any good-quality creamy blue cheese will work in this dish.

Combine the vinegar, shallots, salt, pepper, sugar, bay leaf, thyme, and garlic in a medium bowl and let stand for 20 minutes. Discard the bay leaf.

Meanwhile, divide the hearts of romaine among individual plates. When ready to serve, slowly whisk the oil into the vinegar mixture and pour over the romaine. Crumble the blue cheese over the top, and serve.

SERVES 8

3 tablespoons **red wine vinegar**

3 **shallots**, coarsely chopped

2 teaspoons **salt**

½ teaspoon freshly ground **black pepper**

½ teaspoon **sugar**

1 **bay leaf**

1 tablespoon finely chopped fresh **thyme**

1 clove **garlic**, crushed

8 **hearts of romaine**, quartered lengthwise and tops removed

½ cup **extra virgin olive oil**

8 ounces **Valdeón** or other creamy **blue cheese** such as Cabrales or Gorgonzola

Roasted Artichokes
with Romesco

Here is a nice alternative to the usual way of serving artichokes in America—steamed and accompanied by mayonnaise. In this method, they turn out a little spicy and are tender enough for most of the vegetable to be eaten. With some crusty bread or a potato or two, it is practically a meal in itself.

Trim the top third from each artichoke. With kitchen shears, trim the thorns from the bottom leaves, and trim off most of the stem. Split each artichoke into 4 wedges. Place them in a large pot with 2 tablespoons of the salt, the peppercorns, mustard seed, bay leaf, chile flakes, thyme, garlic, ¼ cup of the oil, and water to cover. Cut the lemon in half, squeeze the juice into the pot, and drop in the lemon. Cover and bring to a boil over high heat. Turn the heat down to medium and simmer until you can easily remove a leaf from the heart of an artichoke, about 25 minutes. (You should err on the undercooked side, as the artichokes will be cooked again.) Drain the artichokes and spread them out evenly to cool.

Preheat the oven to 375°F. Once the artichokes are cool enough to handle, gently clean out the fibrous choke and center leaves with your fingers and discard. In a large bowl, toss the artichokes with the remaining 1 tablespoon salt, the pepper, and the remaining ½ cup oil. Spread them out evenly on a sheet pan with the heart side up. Roast until the artichokes are golden brown, about 25 minutes. Serve with Romesco Sauce.

SERVES 8

8 **artichokes**

3 tablespoons **salt**

1 teaspoon **black peppercorns**

1 teaspoon **mustard seed**

1 **bay leaf**

2 teaspoons **dried red chile flakes**

6 sprigs **thyme**

4 cloves **garlic**, crushed

¾ cup **extra virgin olive oil**

1 **lemon**

1 teaspoon freshly ground **black pepper**

Romesco Sauce (page 196)

Roasted New Potatoes
with Romesco

SERVES 8

24 **Yukon Gold potatoes** or
red new potatoes

Salt and freshly ground **black pepper**

½ cup **extra virgin olive oil**

Romesco Sauce (page 196)

We use this method to cook our potatoes—letting them finish cooking in the residual heat of boiled water—because it prevents the skins from bursting open. Roasting them afterward makes them wonderfully crisp on the outside and tender on the inside. Look for Yukon Gold potatoes or other small, waxy heirloom varieties.

Place the potatoes in a large pot with salted water to cover, and bring to a rapid boil. Cover immediately with a tight-fitting lid, remove from the heat, and let the potatoes finish cooking in the residual heat until you can easily pierce them with a paring knife, about 1 hour. Drain and let cool. Cut the potatoes in half.

Preheat the oven to 400°F. Line a sheet pan with parchment paper. Toss the potatoes in a large bowl with the oil and season with salt and pepper. Spread them skin side down on the sheet pan and roast until they are crisp on the outside and have a roasted color, about 15 minutes. Serve with Romesco Sauce.

Roasted Eggplant
with Romesco

SERVES 8

2 **eggplants**, tops and bottoms
trimmed and cut lengthwise into 8
wedges

1 tablespoon **salt**

1 teaspoon freshly ground
 black pepper

½ cup **extra virgin olive oil**

Romesco Sauce (page 196)

We also use this eggplant to make the bocadillo *(sandwich) known as* escalivada *(page 168). After they are cooked, the eggplants should be very soft and succulent, with no toughness left in the skins, and have a caramel-like sweetness.*

Preheat the oven to 400°F. Line a sheet pan with parchment paper. Toss the eggplants in a large bowl with the salt, pepper, and oil. Place the wedges skin side down on the sheet pan and roast until they are soft, spongy, and have a rich, roasted color, about 40 minutes. Serve with Romesco Sauce.

Grilled Spring Onions
with Romesco

A much-anticipated ritual takes place in Catalonia when the local green onions known as calçots *first appear in the spring. Restaurants and home cooks alike grill the onions and stand, cloaked in protective bibs, to feast on them. Holding the leaf end of the onion, they sensuously peel away the outer skin, whereupon they draw the onion through the* romesco *sauce, hold it aloft, and slowly and delicately lower it into the mouth. Who says food can't be sexy?*

Light a fire in a charcoal grill or heat a stovetop grill. Trim the roots from the onions, pull off any dry outer leaves, and rinse and dry thoroughly. Toss the onions in a large bowl with the oil and season with salt and pepper. Place over the hot grill, turning as needed, until lightly charred, about 5 minutes (a minute or two less if using scallions). Wrap in newspaper or a paper bag for 5 minutes to let the residual heat steam the onions through. Serve with Romesco Sauce.

SERVES 8

16 **spring onions** or **scallions**
⅓ cup **extra virgin olive oil**
Salt and freshly ground **black pepper**
Romesco Sauce (page 196)

Escarole Salad

SERVES 8

1 large or 2 small heads **escarole**

¾ cup **extra virgin olive oil**

6 cloves **garlic**, finely chopped

2 tablespoons **sherry vinegar**

1 teaspoon **salt**

½ teaspoon freshly ground **black pepper**

1 tablespoon **sugar**

24 **black olives**, pitted

Escarole is a hearty green that isn't used as much as it deserves to be. Sometimes called batavia and related to curly endive (chicory), it has a bold flavor and a heart of white leaves tinged with yellow at the edges. It is most often used raw in salads, but it also wilts very nicely in hot vinaigrette. This salad is no wallflower, but rather an assertive, deliciously effusive dish with an enticing hint of garlic and sherry.

Remove the outer leaves and any discolored or ragged tops of the escarole. Tear the leaves into bite-sized pieces, and wash and dry thoroughly. Place in a large bowl.

Heat half of the oil in a skillet over medium-high heat. Add the garlic and cook until it begins to color, then remove the pan from the heat and allow the garlic to continue to cook for several seconds to a golden brown. Lightly whisk the remaining oil, the vinegar, salt, pepper, and sugar into the hot pan. Pour the hot vinaigrette over the escarole leaves and toss well. Serve immediately, with the olives scattered on top.

Mushrooms al Ajillo

Half of the appeal of this dish is the chance to dip good, crusty bread into the flavorful oil. Of course, the mushrooms are excellent, too. This is great cocktail food, in that a good, astringent alcohol helps cut the oil. Cook the mushrooms right before serving, and make sure they are swimming in the hot oil, ready to be soaked up with bread. We also make this dish with shrimp; simply substitute shrimp for the mushrooms (or use both), and cook just until the shrimp turn opaque.

Heat the oil to 375°F in a heavy-bottomed pan or cast-iron skillet. Place individual *cazuelas* (terra-cotta casseroles) or ramekins, or 1 large casserole dish, into a warm oven. Add the garlic to the oil and fry just until it begins to turn golden, about 1½ minutes (it will continue to cook after it comes out of the oil). Remove the garlic with a skimmer and place on paper towels. Add the chiles to the oil and fry just until the oil begins to bubble up around them, about 10 seconds; they should still be slightly chewy. Remove the chiles with a skimmer and set aside with the garlic. Season the mushrooms with salt and pepper and put them in the oil. Fry until tender, about 2 minutes. Return the garlic and chiles to the pan and stir in the parsley. Immediately remove from the heat and transfer to the warmed dish(es). Serve at once with lots of crusty bread.

SERVES 8

2 cups **extra virgin olive oil**

8 cloves **garlic**, thinly sliced

2 **guajillo chiles**, stems removed and sliced into thin rings

4 cups **button** or **cremini mushrooms**, quartered

Salt and freshly ground **black pepper**

Handful of fresh **flat-leaf parsley leaves**, chopped

Beet Salad
with Anise Seed Vinaigrette

SERVES 8

Beets

1 pound **beets**, without the tops

1 **bay leaf**

4 cloves **garlic**, crushed

½ bunch **thyme**

1 teaspoon **black peppercorns**

½ cup **extra virgin olive oil**

Salt

Vinaigrette

1 **yellow onion**, diced

2 teaspoons **salt**

¼ cup **red wine vinegar**

1 tablespoon **anise seed**, crushed
with a mortar and pestle

½ teaspoon freshly ground
black pepper

1 teaspoon **sugar**

½ cup **extra virgin olive oil**

1 small bulb **fennel**, sliced paper-thin

2 tablespoons **Herb Oil** (page 198)

1 tablespoon freshly squeezed
lemon juice

Salt

1 bunch **arugula**, tough stems
removed

Beets always seem to work best in a salad, with borscht perhaps the only exception. They like to be dressed, and they are bold enough to stand up to a flavorful dressing such as our anise seed vinaigrette. An advantage to this salad is that it is best at room temperature, and much of the work can be finished before the guests arrive.

Preheat the oven to 425°F. Combine the beets, bay leaf, garlic, thyme, peppercorns, and oil in a large bowl, season with salt, and toss together. Place the coated beets in a roasting pan and cover with foil. Roast until you can easily pierce the beets with a knife, about 1 hour. Set aside to cool.

While the beets are cooling, prepare the vinaigrette. Toss the onion and salt in a medium bowl and let stand for 10 minutes. Whisk in the vinegar, anise seed, pepper, and sugar, and let stand for 30 minutes. Slowly whisk in the oil.

When the beets are cool enough to handle, slip off the skins and discard. (If they don't slip off easily, the beets did not cook long enough.) Cut into bite-sized wedges. Add to the vinaigrette and toss to coat evenly.

In a separate bowl, toss together the fennel, Herb Oil, lemon juice, and salt to taste.

To assemble the salad, arrange a small bed of arugula on individual plates and pile the dressed beets on top. Top the beets with the dressed fennel and serve.

Poached Salmon
with Cilantro and Cumin Vinaigrette

This is a lovely, full-flavored salad that could easily be a meal by itself. The method for poaching the fish is unusual but highly effective. For convenience, the fish can be poached up to a day in advance. You will probably have leftover vinaigrette, which can be stored in a jar and used for other salads.

Cut the salmon into 1-inch squares and arrange in a single layer, with space between the pieces, in a nonreactive baking pan. If you have thicker and thinner pieces, divide them between 2 pans so you can time the cooking correctly.

To poach the salmon, in a medium saucepan, combine the wine, peppercorns, jalapeño, onion, and parsley, and bring to a boil. Pour the boiling liquid through a sieve directly over the salmon. Cover tightly. After 2 minutes (3 minutes for pieces thicker than 1 inch), drain off the liquid and put the fish in the refrigerator to cool. It should be perfectly cooked, slightly rosy in the middle, after chilling. After it is completely cool, cover the fish. You can prepare the fish up to this point a day in advance.

To make the vinaigrette, combine the jalapeño and vinegar in a small saucepan and bring almost to a boil over medium-high heat. Remove from the heat and let cool completely, allowing the chile to infuse the vinegar. Add the lime juice and whisk in the oil. Add the cumin seed, salt, pepper, and garlic, and whisk it all together.

To assemble the salad, toss the cilantro in a medium bowl with enough of the vinaigrette to coat it lightly. Make a loose bed of the greens on individual plates. Tuck the poached salmon in among the leaves and top each salmon piece with a dollop of Mojo Verde.

SERVES 8

Poached Salmon

2 pounds **salmon fillets**, skinned and pin bones removed

2 cups **dry white wine**

1½ teaspoons **black peppercorns**

1 **jalapeño chile**, cut in half lengthwise

½ **white onion**, thinly sliced

5 sprigs **flat-leaf parsley**

Vinaigrette

1 **jalapeño chile**, sliced into thin rings

2 tablespoons **white wine vinegar**

3 tablespoons freshly squeezed **lime juice**

¾ cup **extra virgin olive oil**

1 tablespoon **cumin seed**, toasted and ground (see page 199)

1 teaspoon **salt**

½ teaspoon freshly ground **black pepper**

2 cloves **garlic**, crushed

1 bunch **cilantro**, tough stems removed

Mojo Verde (page 197)

Rice & Fideos

Forget all those side orders of Spanish rice you've had. Rice cooking in Spain, especially in the rice-growing regions of Valencia and Murcia, is an art form, and the details and nuances are hotly contested among the cognoscenti. Like so many other ingredients, rice was brought to Spain by the Moors, who found in the fertile marshlands of the Albufera lagoon near the city of Valencia the ideal conditions for cultivating their staple food. Although this is the most famous rice-growing region in Europe, and the home of one of the all-time great rice dishes, paella, many passionate rice lovers insist that the best rice comes from the inland marshes around Calasparra in Murcia, fed by the Segura River. Either way, the rice to look for is short-grain and starchy, and can absorb large amounts of liquid much like the varieties used in Italy for risotto.

Pasta came to Spain with the Romans through the port city of Barcelona, and it is here that it still reaches its culinary apex in Spain. Although pasta is also popular throughout the Mediterranean coast of Valencia, where it sometimes even supplants rice in traditional paellas, the most singular use of it is in the toasted *fideos* beloved by Catalans.

On the César menu, these two staples, rice and pasta, are represented mainly by paella and *fideos negro,* two uniquely Spanish dishes that are also cherished by American diners. Neither recipe is meant to be the definitive rendition of that dish, just our version of a well-loved classic.

Chef Maggie Pond sits in a large paella dish.

Paella César

SERVES 8 (TAPA-SIZED PORTIONS)

Chicken Drumettes

2 tablespoons **extra virgin olive oil**

1 tablespoon **Moruño Spice**
(page 199)

1 teaspoon finely chopped **garlic**

2 teaspoons freshly squeezed **lemon juice**

1 teaspoon **salt**

8 **chicken drumettes** (the uppermost part of the wing)

Paella

¼ cup **extra virgin olive oil**

8 ounces **Chorizo** (page 139), sliced (about two 5-inch links)

4 cups **short-grain rice**

½ cup **Sofrito** (page 198)

8 cups **Shellfish Stock** (page 201), bottled **clam juice**, or **Roasted Chicken Stock** (page 202)

3 tablespoons **salt**

16 **Manila clams**, scrubbed

16 **black mussels**, scrubbed

8 large **shrimp** (8 to 10 ounces), shells on

½ cup fresh **English peas**, blanched for 30 seconds in boiling salted water

½ cup **piquillo peppers** (see page 87), cut into ¼-inch julienne

1 **lemon**, cut into 8 wedges

Alioli (page 195)

Paella is the best-known dish from Spain and is considered even by most Spaniards to be the national dish. Despite its association with seafood, paella was probably first made by inland farmers who cooked it in the fields over open fires with vegetables, snails, and, if they were lucky, rabbit. Later, chicken and sausages were added to the mélange, and eventually the coastal rice growers picked up on the idea and produced paella marinara *with fish and shellfish instead of meat. Ultimately, the concept of* paella mixta *developed, combining land and sea creatures, as does this paella that we serve at César. Paella pans are inexpensive and come in many sizes, and they are well worth the minor investment. This recipe is designed for a 15- to 16-inch paella pan, but it could easily be increased to accommodate larger pans and larger crowds. You can serve it in tapa-sized portions or follow the tradition of placing the pan in the center of the table and giving everyone a wooden spoon for digging in.*

To prepare the drumettes, whisk together the oil, Moruño Spice, garlic, lemon juice, and salt in a medium bowl. Toss with the chicken, cover, and refrigerate for at least 2 hours, or preferably overnight. Preheat the oven to 375°F. Roast the chicken until golden brown and crispy, about 25 minutes. The pieces should cook through only about 75 percent, as they will be cooked again.

To make the paella, heat a paella pan over medium-high heat. Add the oil, completely coating the pan. Add the Chorizo and sauté until it begins to render out some of its fat, about 1 minute. Add the rice and sauté for 2 minutes, stirring occasionally. Add the Sofrito and stir to completely coat the rice. Spread the rice out evenly in the pan and add the stock. Sprinkle the salt evenly over the paella and distribute the drumettes around the outermost part of the pan. Once the stock comes to a boil, turn the heat down to a simmer and add the shellfish, distributing them evenly in the pan. Once the rice has absorbed about 95 percent of the stock, after about 20 minutes, add the peas and *piquillo* peppers. Continue to cook until all the stock is absorbed, about 5 minutes longer. Discard any mussels or clams that haven't opened. Garnish with the lemon wedges and serve with the Alioli.

Fideos Negro

SERVES 8 (TAPA-SIZED PORTIONS)

1 cup **extra virgin olive oil**

4 cups **fideos** (about 1 pound) or other thin pasta broken into small pieces

$\frac{1}{3}$ cup **Sofrito** (page 198)

1 teaspoon (1 envelope) **squid ink**

4 **squid**, cleaned (see page 203), bodies cut into $\frac{1}{2}$-inch rings, and tentacles left whole

$4\frac{1}{2}$ cups **Shellfish Stock** (page 201)

2 teaspoons **salt**

16 large **shrimp** (about 1 pound), shells on

16 **Manila clams**, scrubbed

$\frac{1}{2}$ cup fresh **English peas**, blanched for 1 minute in boiling salted water

$\frac{1}{2}$ cup **piquillo peppers** (see page 87), cut into $\frac{1}{4}$-inch julienne

1 **lemon**, cut into 8 wedges

Alioli (page 195)

Fideos, or fideus in Catalan, is a holdover from the Moorish term for pasta, specifically any thin pasta such as vermicelli or angel hair. The act of frying or toasting the pasta is said to be unique to Catalonia in Spain and Apulia in southern Italy, evidence that the technique might be a Roman inspiration. Fideos are also used both in Italy and Latin America, but typically in soups without being toasted first. Consequently, fideos can often be found in Latin markets. If not, you can use any long, thin pasta and break it up into small pieces. (Ultimately, think of fideos more as rice than pasta in terms of cooking.) The use of squid ink to color both rice and pasta dishes is quite common in Catalonia. Fideos are traditionally cooked in a pan called a cazuela, a flameproof casserole made of terra-cotta. If you don't have one, use a paella pan.

In a heavy-bottomed 1-quart saucepan, heat the oil to 350°F. Add the *fideos* and fry until they turn an orange-brown, about 8 minutes. Drain the noodles, reserving $\frac{1}{4}$ cup of the oil.

Heat a 13-inch *cazuela* or paella pan over medium-high heat. Add the reserved oil and coat the pan completely. Add the *fideos*, Sofrito, and squid ink, and sauté for 2 minutes. Stir in the squid and spread the *fideos* out evenly in the pan. Add the stock and sprinkle the salt evenly over the surface. Once the stock comes to a boil, turn the heat down to a simmer and add the shrimp and clams, distributing them evenly in the pan. Once the *fideos* have absorbed about 95 percent of the stock, after about 10 minutes, add the peas and *piquillos*. Continue to cook until all the stock is absorbed, about 3 minutes longer. Discard any clams that haven't opened. Garnish with the lemon wedges and serve with the Alioli.

Croquetas de Arroz con Jamón y Yerbas

These flavorful little rice balls with ham and herbs take a bit of work to make but can be prepared up to a day ahead of time and kept in the refrigerator until you are ready to fry them. They make great party food since they're small and not too messy. Using a #60 (1-ounce) ice-cream scoop makes this job faster and the size of the balls more consistent. The balls are also fun to make with a group or, as we've discovered, with kids.

Line 2 sheet pans with parchment paper. Heat the olive oil over medium-high heat in a large, heavy-bottomed saucepan. Add the rice and cook until translucent, about 1 minute. Add the garlic and cook for 1 minute more. Add half of the lemon zest, the thyme, bay leaf, salt, pepper, and water, and bring to a boil. Cover, turn the heat down to low, and simmer until the water is absorbed, about 15 minutes. Spread the rice on 1 sheet pan, discard the bay leaf, and allow the rice to cool.

In a large bowl, mix the rice with the *jamón*, parsley, chives, and the remainder of the lemon zest. Using a 1-ounce ice-cream scoop, form the mixture into firm balls about 1 inch in diameter. Place the flour, eggs, and bread crumbs in 3 separate wide, shallow bowls. Working in batches of 6 to 8 balls, dust them first in the flour, shake off any excess, coat them in the egg, and finally roll them in the bread crumbs. Place them on the second prepared pan. Repeat until all of the rice balls are breaded. At this point they can be covered and refrigerated for up to 1 day before frying them.

In a large, deep pot, heat the peanut oil to 375°F. Fry the rice balls in small batches until they are golden brown, about 1 minute. Scoop them out with a long-handled skimmer, and drain on paper towels. Serve immediately.

MAKES ABOUT 60 CROQUETAS

2 tablespoons **extra virgin olive oil**

2 cups **short-grain rice**

2 cloves **garlic**, minced

Zest of 2 **lemons**

1 tablespoon chopped fresh **thyme**

1 **bay leaf**

2 teaspoons **salt**

1½ teaspoons freshly ground **black pepper**

3 cups **water**

1 cup finely chopped or ground **jamón serrano** (about 12 slices)

3 tablespoons finely chopped fresh **flat-leaf parsley**

¼ cup finely chopped fresh **chives**

2 cups **all-purpose flour**, seasoned with salt and black pepper

4 **eggs**, whisked and seasoned with salt and black pepper

4 cups **bread crumbs** from a day-old sweet baguette

4 cups **peanut oil**

Potatoes

Our potato tapas have always been in great demand at César. Once, during a local street festival held out in front of César, we set up a large wok with hot oil and had someone turning out *papas fritas* all afternoon, much to the delight of hundreds of Berkeley denizens. Salty, starchy, sometimes spicy, and usually accompanied by *alioli* or another sauce, these potato dishes provide a perfect complement to all sorts of cocktails, beer, and wine. Although we've indicated specific quantities of potatoes in the recipes, you can adjust them to make as much as you will need for the number of people you expect. For the fried recipes, the amount of oil stays the same since you want to fry only a handful of potatoes at a time to prevent the oil temperature from dropping.

Patatas Bravas

Wrinkled New Potatoes

Papas Fritas with Cumin, Garlic, and Alioli

Homemade Potato Chips with Gallega Spice

Fried Potatoes with Herbs and Sea Salt

Patatas Bravas

Brava Sauce

¼ cup **extra virgin olive oil**

1 **yellow onion**, thinly sliced

1 clove **garlic**, thinly sliced

1 **guajillo chile**, stem removed

2 tablespoons **dried red chile flakes**

4 cups canned **tomatoes**, drained

½ cup **sugar**

¾ cup **distilled white vinegar**

¼ cup **dry white wine**

1 **bay leaf**

¼ cup chopped fresh **flat-leaf parsley**

1 teaspoon **salt**

½ teaspoon freshly ground
black pepper

Brava Salt

5 tablespoons **pimentón dulce**
(see page 87)

3 tablespoons **pimentón picante**
(see page 87)

3 tablespoons **paprika**

1 tablespoon **cayenne pepper**

½ cup **salt**

5 **russet potatoes**, each cut lengthwise into 8 wedges

8 cups **peanut oil**

Alioli (page 195)

These fried potatoes are popular in the tapas bars throughout Spain, but especially in Madrid. Because of the similar technique, they can be made in tandem with the Papas Fritas (page 127). Any extra Brava Salt will keep indefinitely, and the sauce will keep in the refrigerator for 2 weeks or the freezer for 2 months.

To make the sauce, heat the oil over medium-high heat in a large, heavy-bottomed pan. Add the onion, turn down the heat to low, and cook slowly until caramelized, about 30 minutes. Add the garlic and cook for another 5 minutes. Add the *guajillo* and chile flakes and simmer for 5 more minutes. Add the tomatoes, sugar, vinegar, white wine, and bay leaf. Simmer, uncovered, until reduced to a thick sauce, about 30 minutes. Put the sauce through a food mill or purée in a food processor. Add the parsley, salt, and pepper. The sauce should have a hot, sweet-and-sour taste. You will have about 3 cups.

To make the salt, combine the *pimentón dulce* and *picante*, paprika, cayenne, and salt in a small bowl. Mix well and set aside.

To fry the potatoes, first soak them in cold water for 15 minutes. Meanwhile, in a large, deep pot, heat the peanut oil to 225°F.

Drain about 8 wedges at a time in a colander and pat dry with paper towels. Drop the potatoes into the hot oil and fry until the tip of a paring knife easily pierces them, about 8 minutes. Using a long-handled skimmer, remove the potatoes and put them on paper towels to drain. Repeat with the remaining potatoes, always cooking just a handful at a time so as not to lower the oil temperature.

To finish the potatoes, heat the same oil to 375°F. Drop a handful of the potatoes into the oil as before, and fry until golden brown, 2 to 3 minutes. Remove from the oil, place in a large bowl, and toss with Brava Salt (use about 1 tablespoon per whole potato). Repeat with the rest of the potatoes. Serve with Brava Sauce and Alioli.

Wrinkled New Potatoes

This dish originated in the Canary Islands, a singular and fascinating archipelago off the coast of Morocco. In the past, fresh water was scarce on the islands; this recipe is probably a result of having to cook in sea water, with the potatoes introduced by Spanish explorers returning from South America. Potatoes prepared in this manner are typically eaten out of hand, broken in two and dipped in the sauces.

Place the potatoes in a large pot with plenty of salted water to cover and bring to a rapid boil. Cover immediately with a tight-fitting lid, remove from the heat, and let the potatoes finish cooking in the residual heat until you can easily pierce them with a paring knife, about 1 hour. Drain the potatoes.

Preheat the oven to 400°F. In a large bowl, toss the potatoes with the oil and season with salt and pepper. Spread them out evenly on a sheet pan and roast until the skins are wrinkled, about 10 minutes. Serve with Mojo Verde and Mojo Picón.

SERVES 8

24 to 30 **red new potatoes** or **Yukon Gold potatoes**

½ cup **extra virgin olive oil**

Salt and freshly ground **black pepper**

Mojo Verde (page 197)

Mojo Picón (page 197)

Papas Fritas
with Cumin, Garlic, and Alioli

Although the technique used here is similar to the one for Patatas Bravas (page 124), these lovely reddish potatoes, coated with cumin and other exotic spices and mixed with fried garlic, taste completely different. They are a perennial favorite, especially when paired with a crisp—read high-acid—white wine or, better yet, a cold beer. They also fare nicely with cocktails that have an astringent note, such as those made with gin. The double frying is the secret to any great fries.

Soak the potatoes in cold water for 15 minutes. Meanwhile, in a large, deep pot, heat the oil to 225°F.

Drain about 8 wedges at a time in a colander and pat dry with paper towels. Drop the potatoes and some of the garlic cloves into the hot oil and fry until a paring knife easily pierces the potatoes, about 8 minutes. Using a long-handled skimmer, remove the potatoes and garlic, and put them on paper towels to drain. Repeat with the remaining potatoes and garlic, cooking just a handful at a time so as not to lower the oil temperature.

To finish the potatoes, heat the same oil to 375°F. Drop a handful of the potatoes and garlic into the oil as before, and fry until the potatoes are golden brown, 2 to 3 minutes. Remove from the oil, place in a large bowl, and toss with the Cumin Spice (use about 2 tablespoons per whole potato) and salt to taste. Repeat with the rest of the potatoes and garlic. Serve with Alioli.

SERVES 8

4 **russet potatoes,** each cut lengthwise into 8 wedges

8 cups **peanut oil**

1 head **garlic,** broken into cloves, unpeeled

½ cup **Cumin Spice** (page 199)

Salt

Alioli (page 195)

Homemade Potato Chips
with Gallega Spice

SERVES 8

5 large **russet potatoes**

8 cups **peanut oil**

⅓ cup **Gallega Spice** (page 199)

Salt

Nothing beats freshly made potato chips, and they are one of the quintessential snacks at a bar with drinks. They are also easy to make if you have a mandoline (so named because the motion of slicing on them resembles someone strumming a mandolin—those French!), or hand-held slicing device. The original French models are now about two hundred dollars, and while they are well worth the investment, several inexpensive Japanese versions (such as the Benriner slicer) available today perform equally well. They come with an assortment of blades and can be adjusted for thickness, making them useful for all sorts of culinary needs.

Slice the potatoes to about ¹⁄₁₆ inch thick on a mandoline. Place them in cold water to soak for 20 minutes. Meanwhile, heat the oil in a large, deep pot to 375°F.

Drain the potatoes and spin dry in a salad spinner. Drop a handful of chips at a time into the hot oil and fry, turning them with tongs until they appear crisp, about 2 minutes. Using a long-handled skimmer, remove the potatoes, shaking off the excess oil, and put them in a large bowl. Toss each batch gently with Gallega Spice (use about 1 tablespoon of the spice mix per whole potato) and salt to taste. Repeat the process, a handful of chips at a time, until they are all fried. Let cool to room temperature before serving.

Fried Potatoes
with Herbs and Sea Salt

These potatoes are perhaps the ultimate cocktail accompaniment and one of the most popular dishes at César. One can usually see plates of them lined up, often amid an array of half-empty glasses, with the thin, crisp potatoes spilling out everywhere on the bar. The savory goodness of this dish owes much to the fresh herbs that are transformed by deep-frying. We've often quipped that we could make a fine bar snack with bowls of fried sage and rosemary, enticingly dusted with sea salt. You will want a mandoline for this job—you could grow old trying to slice the potatoes by hand. Notice that because these are so thin, they are fried only once.

SERVES 8

5 **russet potatoes**

1 bunch **sage**

1 bunch **rosemary**

8 cups **peanut oil**

Sea Salt and freshly ground **black pepper**

Alioli (page 195)

Slice the potatoes into thin strips by running them through a mandoline fitted with the $\frac{1}{4}$-inch-wide cross-cut blade adjusted to cut slices $\frac{1}{16}$ inch thick. Place them in cold water to soak for 15 minutes. Meanwhile, remove the herb leaves from their stems and toss them together. Heat the oil to 375° in a large, deep pot.

Drain the potatoes and spin dry in a salad spinner. Drop a handful of potatoes at a time into the hot oil and fry for about 30 seconds. Using a pair of long tongs, scoop up the potatoes, give them a turn, and cook for another minute or so. Once they just begin to turn golden, drop in a handful of the herbs and cook until the herbs have crisped up, another 15 seconds. Using a long-handled skimmer, remove the potatoes and herbs, shaking off the excess oil, and put them in a large bowl. Toss with sea salt and pepper to taste. Repeat the process, a handful of potatoes at a time, until they are all fried. Serve immediately with Alioli.

Meats

Vegetarians have a tough time in Spain. Meat figures prominently on the menus of restaurants throughout the country, often in the form of grilled lamb or beef steak, as well as roasts and stews of various kinds, and it is all consumed with zeal. Our relatively brief selection of meat-based tapas would seem to belie that passion, but in fact, heavier meat dishes tend to be reserved for the main meal, whereas the tapas menu typically focuses more on seafood than meat, with one notable exception: cured pork products in all their many regional varieties. Leading the way is *jamón serrano*, the much beloved air-cured ham that is ubiquitous in tapas bars all over the land, even appearing in roadside truck stops. In fact, one of the most basic, and most popular, tapas is simply a plate of sliced ham, with or without garnishes. Although every region of Spain produces some type of cured or cooked pork sausage, chorizo is without doubt the national sausage, and it figures in all sorts of soups, stews, and paellas, as well as being a featured player on tapas menus. We have tried here to present a group of meat dishes that reflect their proportion on our menu. Being the unabashed carnivores that we are, however, we have been known to bring out a platter of grilled lamb chops that are quickly dispensed with at the bar amid a flurry of napkins.

Cumin Fried Chicken
with Watercress and Blood Orange Alioli

SERVES 8

Blood Orange Alioli

2 cups freshly squeezed **blood orange juice** or regular **orange juice**

1 cup **Alioli** (page 195)

Fried Chicken

2 pounds skinless, boneless **chicken thighs**, cut into bite-sized pieces

1 teaspoon **salt**

1½ cups **buttermilk**

½ cup **Cumin Spice** (page 199)

1 tablespoon **pimentón dulce** (see page 87)

3 cups **all-purpose flour**

Lemon Vinaigrette

2 **shallots**, finely diced

⅓ cup freshly squeezed **lemon juice**

2 teaspoons **salt**

1 teaspoon freshly ground **black pepper**

Pinch of **sugar**

1 **bay leaf**

4 sprigs **thyme**

1¼ cups **extra virgin olive oil**

8 cups **peanut oil**

1 bunch **watercress** or **arugula**, tough stems removed

Most people love fried chicken, and these bite-sized nuggets are perfect for a cocktail party or a casual snack. They are at once mildly spicy and tart from the vinaigrette and the orange-flavored alioli. *We don't use a lot of chicken at César, but this recipe raises it from the mundane to the sublime. Maggie prefers to use thigh meat because it is a little fattier and more flavorful, but you can use breast meat if you like. You can make the* alioli *a day ahead of time and keep it in the refrigerator.*

To make the *alioli*, in a medium saucepan, bring the orange juice to a simmer over medium-high heat and reduce to about ¼ cup, about 15 minutes. Strain into a medium bowl. Let cool slightly, then whisk in the *alioli*. Cover tightly and chill.

To prepare the chicken, combine the chicken, salt, and buttermilk in a small baking dish. Let marinate for at least 30 minutes, or refrigerate and marinate for up to 2 hours.

In a wide, shallow bowl, mix the Cumin Spice and *pimentón* with the flour and set aside. To make the vinaigrette, combine the shallots, lemon juice, salt, pepper, sugar, bay leaf, and thyme in a medium bowl. Slowly whisk in the olive oil, and then let stand for 20 minutes to blend the flavors while you fry the chicken. Discard the bay leaf.

Heat the peanut oil in a large, deep pot to 375°F. Take a few pieces of chicken at a time from the buttermilk and dredge them in the flour mixture. Fry the chicken in small batches (to keep the temperature of the oil from dropping) until it is golden brown, 2 to 3 minutes. Using a long-handled skimmer, remove the chicken to a heatproof platter and keep in a warm oven while you continue to cook the remaining chicken and prepare the salad.

In a large bowl, toss the watercress with the vinaigrette. Divide among individual plates and top with the chicken. Serve the Blood Orange Alioli on the side for dipping.

Lamb Meatballs in Almond Sauce

Almond Sauce

6 tablespoons **extra virgin olive oil**

4 **yellow onions**, finely diced

12 cloves **garlic**, thinly sliced

1 cup **dry white wine**

5 cups **Roasted Chicken Stock** (page 202)

1 **bay leaf**

1/4 teaspoon **saffron threads**

2 teaspoons **salt**

1/8 teaspoon **cayenne pepper**

3 cups finely diced **carrots**

1 1/2 cups **blanched almonds**, ground (about 1 cup)

Meatballs

1/4 cup **dry red wine** such as Rioja

1 cup **bread crumbs** from a day-old sweet baguette

2 pounds **ground lamb**

2 **eggs**

1 1/2 tablespoons freshly ground **black pepper**

4 cloves **garlic**

1 1/2 tablespoons **salt**

This recipe was adapted from The Foods & Wines of Spain *by Penelope Casas, the first comprehensive book on Spanish cuisine in English. Casas has been an inspiration to César from the beginning, and we continue to learn from her books and articles. This dish uses four favorite ingredients in Spain—lamb, red wine, almonds (which act as a thickener in the sauce), and garlic—resulting in a hearty, satisfying stew. Bring on those big, bad Rioja reds.*

To make the sauce, heat the oil over medium-high heat in a large saucepan. Add the onions and sauté until they are soft and translucent, about 10 minutes. Add the garlic and sauté for 5 more minutes. Deglaze the pan with the wine, scraping up the browned bits from the pan bottom, then boil until reduced by one-fourth, about 2 minutes. Add the stock, bay leaf, saffron, salt, and cayenne, and simmer for 5 minutes. Add the carrots and almonds, and simmer for another 10 minutes. Set aside.

To make the meatballs, preheat the oven to 375°F. Line a sheet pan with parchment paper. In a large bowl, pour the red wine over the bread crumbs and let soak for 2 minutes. Add the lamb, eggs, and pepper. Using a mortar and pestle, pound the garlic and salt to a paste, then add it to the meat mixture. Mix well. Use a #60 (1-ounce) ice-cream scoop to scoop up a meatball about 1 inch in diameter and place on the sheet pan. Repeat with the remaining meat mixture, placing the meatballs 1/2 inch apart. Bake for 10 minutes.

Add the meatballs to the almond sauce, return to medium heat, and simmer for 5 minutes. Serve immediately.

Empanadillas
with Pork Filling and Pimentón Dough

Empanadas, which are now ubiquitous throughout Spain and Latin America, are originally from the region of Galicia in northwest Spain. They figure into the traditions of the pilgrims who sojourn to Santiago de Compostela, and their image (in the crescent form) is even carved into the great cathedral there. It is said that any pilgrim who eats one in the cathedral (in which the remains of the disciple Saint James are said to lie) will have an eternity of joy equal to the pleasure of eating this tasty pastry.

Empanadas are basically meat pies, although they can also be made with vegetables or whatever is leftover in the kitchen. Empanadillas, *as the name implies, are little versions of the pastry, typically formed into crescents. It is in this shape that they are most often seen in Mexico and elsewhere in Latin America, usually at holiday celebrations. Whether they are full-sized pies, cut up into pieces, or formed into individual crescents, they are popular tapa fare throughout Spain.*

This is a good dish to make with a group, or you can make the dough in advance and freeze it so you can make the pastries anytime. The dough was adapted from a recipe in Barbara Tropp's marvelous China Moon Cookbook. *China is admittedly a far cry from Iberia, but the dough works perfectly for this savory pastry. In Spain, the dough is usually made with lard, but we have substituted vegetable shortening since most American cooks don't keep lard in the pantry. Feel free to use lard if you have it. The quantity may seem like a lot, but* empanadillas *freeze well, and if you are serving these at a party, you'll find they go very quickly.*

MAKES ABOUT FORTY 4-INCH
EMPANADILLAS

Pimentón Dough

¾ cup (1½ sticks) **unsalted butter**,
chilled

¼ cup **vegetable shortening**

3 cups **all-purpose flour**

2 tablespoons **sugar**

Pinch of **salt**

3 tablespoons **Gallega Spice** (page 199)

⅔ to ¾ cup **ice water**

Pork Filling

2 tablespoons **extra virgin olive oil**

2 **yellow onions**, finely diced

1 teaspoon minced **garlic**

¾ pound **ground pork**

½ cup diced **piquillo peppers**
(see page 87)

1 tablespoon finely chopped fresh
flat-leaf parsley

1 tablespoon **Gallega Spice** (page 199)

1 tablespoon **salt**

⅛ teaspoon freshly ground
black pepper

⅛ teaspoon ground **cinnamon**

Grated **zest of 1 orange**

1 **egg yolk**

2 tablespoons **heavy cream**

To make the dough, combine the butter, shortening, flour, sugar, salt, and Gallega Spice in a food processor. Pulse until the mixture resembles coarse meal. With the machine running, add the ice water, a little bit at a time. Stop when the dough just clumps together, almost forming a ball. Turn the dough out onto a lightly floured board and divide in half. Press each half into a 1-inch-thick disk and wrap in plastic wrap. Refrigerate for at least 1 hour before rolling out the dough. (At this point, the dough can be frozen for up to 2 weeks.)

To make the pork filling, heat the oil in a large sauté pan over medium-high heat. Add the onions and sauté until soft and translucent, about 10 minutes. Add the garlic and cook for another minute. Add the pork and cook, stirring frequently, until it is completely browned, about 5 minutes. Add the *piquillos*, parsley, Gallega Spice, salt, pepper, and cinnamon, and cook for another 5 minutes. Remove from the heat and drain off any excess liquid. Stir in the orange zest. Allow to cool completely before filling the pastry.

To fill and bake the *empanadillas*, using 1 disk at a time, roll out the cold dough on a lightly floured board to an even thickness of about ⅛ inch. Using a 4-inch-round cookie cutter, cut out as many circles as you can. Reroll the scraps and cut more circles. If the dough scraps get too warm, chill them before rerolling.

Preheat the oven to 350°F. Line 2 sheet pans with parchment paper. Place 2 teaspoons of the filling just off center on a circle of dough. Dip a finger in cold water and run it around the edge of the pastry to act as glue when you press the two sides together. Fold over the circle to form a half moon. To seal the pastry, crimp the edges with a fork. Repeat for the rest of the filling and dough.

Lay the filled pastries on the sheet pans, spacing them about 1 inch apart. Whisk together the egg yolk and cream, and lightly brush a thin layer of the wash on each pastry. Bake until golden brown, about 15 minutes. They taste best when allowed to cool slightly to just above room temperature.

Chorizo

Chorizo is the national sausage of Spain, and indeed, it is synonymous with sausage there. Although it is believed to have originated in the far western region of Extremadura, versions are made in every part of the country, as well as in neighboring Portugal. Chorizo crossed the ocean to become the de facto sausage of Mexico and much of Central and South America, a curious development considering that the New World chile gives chorizo its distinctive color and taste. The flavors of paprika and pimentón pervade Spanish-style chorizo, accented by garlic, salt, and herbs. Chorizo made in Latin America or the United States commonly uses a variety of fresh chiles, such as serrano and jalapeño, as well as spices like cumin and coriander. If you have a meat grinder or an appropriate attachment for your mixer, it is well worth it to make our full-flavored, spicy version for the recipes in this book or to cook on its own. Casings come either packed in salt, in which case they need to be flushed out before using, or preflushed and packed in Cryovac, the way ours come.

MAKES ABOUT 48 SMALL OR
12 LARGE SAUSAGES

2 **guajillo chiles**, stems removed

½ cup **water**

3 pounds **pork butt**

2 cups peeled **garlic** cloves

2 tablespoons **salt**

1 ½ teaspoons **black peppercorns**

2 tablespoons **paprika**

1½ teaspoons **cayenne pepper**

3 tablespoons **pimentón dulce**
(see page 87)

1 tablespoon **pimentón picante**
(see page 87)

6 feet medium **hog casing**

Place the *guajillo* chiles and water in a small saucepan and simmer over medium heat for 5 minutes. Let the chiles cool in their cooking water for at least 1 hour or for up to overnight. Reserve ¼ cup of the chile cooking liquid.

Cut the pork into strips, removing any tough tendons, and run it through a meat grinder on the coarse setting. Set aside.

Place the garlic, salt, and chiles in the bowl of a food processor and chop very finely. Stop the motor occasionally and scrape down the sides of the bowl. Add the peppercorns, paprika, cayenne, *pimentón dulce* and *picante,* and the reserved chile liquid and process to a paste. Add this spice mixture to the ground pork and mix it into the meat well. Refrigerate overnight.

To stuff the sausage, set up the meat grinder with a sausage horn, omitting the cutting blade or plate. Slip the clean hog casing onto the horn, leaving 3 or 4 inches dangling. Begin feeding the pork mixture into the meat grinder and gently hold the casing on the horn until it begins to fill with meat. Slowly and gently let it slip off the horn as it fills. Don't overfill, as the casing will break during the linking and cooking.

For Migas or Paella

Twist into 5-inch lengths, hang from a clean rod in a cool, dark place, and let air-dry for 7 days. Layer loosely in paper towels and refrigerate for up to 2 months.

For Chorizo and Apples in Hard Cider

Twist into 1-inch lengths and refrigerate overnight before using. They will keep in the refrigerator for 5 to 7 days.

Chorizo and Apples in Hard Cider

Sidra, *or hard apple cider, is the regional drink of Asturias in northwestern Spain, home to hearty stews and boldly flavored cheese.* Sidra *is consumed in a curious ritual that dates back centuries. You stand with the bottle raised in your hand, over the top of your head, while the pint glass is held low at arm's length alongside the thigh. It is important that the cider falls in a steady stream down to the glass, resulting in a burst of foam that is the very essence of the drink. Apples and pork seem to go together naturally, and this regional dish grew from the love of both in a land famous for its apples. This is a great tapa for the fall months when a chill begins to fill the air and the apples are at their best.*

In a large Dutch oven or traditional *cazuela* (a flameproof terra-cotta casserole), combine the chorizo, apples, and cider. Bring to a boil and then turn the heat down to a simmer and cook until the apples are tender and the sausages are cooked through, about 30 minutes. Remove the apples and chorizo from the pan. Continue to cook the cider down to a thick syrup, reducing it to $\frac{1}{2}$ cup, about 5 minutes. Return the chorizo and apples to the pan, reheating and glazing them with the reduced cider syrup. Serve immediately.

SERVES 8

16 small (1-inch) links **chorizo** (page 139)

2 **Gala apples**, cored and each cut into about 16 cubes

2 cups **hard cider**

Migas
with Chorizo, Peppers, and Fried Eggs

SERVES 6

Fried Peppers

Extra virgin olive oil, for frying

1 **red bell pepper,** seeded and cut into ¼-inch julienne

2 **Anaheim chiles,** seeded and cut into ¼-inch julienne

Salt and freshly ground **black pepper**

Migas

⅓ cup **extra virgin olive oil**

3 **yellow onions,** diced

4 teaspoons finely chopped **garlic**

5 ounces **Chorizo** (page 139), cut into ¼-inch cubes (about 1½ 5-inch links)

1 tablespoon **Gallega Spice** (page 199)

3 cups **bread crumbs** from a day-old sweet baguette

Salt and freshly **ground pepper**

Extra virgin olive oil, for frying

6 **eggs**

Migas *was born on the vast, harsh Spanish plains, created by the shepherds who sometimes had little more than stale bread, wild garlic, olive oil, and, if they were lucky, peppers. Even today, shepherds out with their flocks will cook up huge batches of* migas *over an open fire in a giant pan that looks like a cross between a paella pan and a wok. Our version makes individual portions with the luxurious addition of chorizo and fried eggs. The eggs must be cooked quickly and efficiently; you may want to practice a couple of times before you make the dish for company. Think of our version of* migas *as an Old World predecessor of* huevos rancheros.

To make the peppers, heat ¼ inch oil in a large sauté pan over high heat until drops of water sizzle. Quickly fry the pepper strips in small batches until the skins begin to blister and brown slightly, about 2 minutes. Using a skimmer, transfer to a colander to drain. Season with salt and pepper

To make the *migas,* heat the oil over medium-high heat in a large, heavy-bottomed pan and add the onions. Cover and cook until the onions are translucent, about 5 minutes. Uncover, add the garlic, and cook for 2 minutes more. Add the chorizo and cook until it gives off most of its oil, about 3 minutes. Add the Gallega Spice and cook for 2 minutes more. Stir in the bread crumbs, making sure they absorb all the juices from the pan, and cook until the mixture is lightly toasted, about 10 minutes. Season with salt and pepper to taste. Divide the mixture among 6 individual *cazuelas* (terra-cotta casseroles) or other shallow, oven-proof dishes and garnish with the peppers, tucking them in and around the bread crumb mixture. Keep in a warm oven while you cook the eggs or, if made ahead, reheat in a 250°F oven just before you cook the eggs.

To cook the eggs, in a small nonstick pan, heat ⅛ inch oil over high heat to the smoking point. Break 1 egg into the hot oil. Season with salt and pepper. Working very quickly, fold in the edge of the egg white with a heat-resistant rubber spatula or wooden spoon. Then spoon some of the hot oil over the egg so that it puffs up and crisps around the edges. All of this must be done in a matter of seconds so that the yolk remains soft. Using a slotted spoon, remove the egg and place it on top of a hot *migas*. Repeat for each serving. Serve immediately.

Jamón Serrano
with Roasted Grapes or Grilled or Fresh Fruit

Thin slices of buttery jamón serrano *(see page 88), the great air-cured ham from Spain, are one of the most common and most basic of tapas. Laid out simply on a plate and washed down with a glass of fino sherry or a cold beer,* jamón serrano *is the classic representation of the taste of Spain. In Spain, the ham is always carved by hand off the leg, which is usually visible sticking up from behind the counter, hoof attached. However, you can have it sliced for you at your local deli, and you can substitute Italian prosciutto if you can't find Spanish* jamón. *At César, good Spanish ham is a standard menu item, drizzled with a bit of olive oil and accompanied by our own assortment of garnishes, depending on the season. Fruit, either raw or cooked, is a classic match for the succulent ham, with grapes, figs, persimmons, and melon being some of our favorites; grilled onions are also a good pairing (see page 109). The four recipes that follow are all designed to accompany* jamón serrano. *In each case, lay out a few slices of ham next to the desired fruit.*

Roasted Grapes

Preheat the oven to 425°F. Line a sheet pan with parchment paper. Lay out several small bunches of Red Flame or other sweet red seedless grapes evenly on the pan. Drizzle sherry vinegar over them and roast for 25 minutes to 1 hour, depending on how much sugar is in the grapes. Halfway through, move the bunches around and flip them. The grapes should start to soften, and some will begin to caramelize. It's all right if they are at varying stages of doneness—some will be fully cooked, some almost burned.

Grilled Figs

Cut the figs in half lengthwise, drizzle with olive oil, and grill over a hot fire for 30 seconds on each side.

Grilled Pears or Persimmons

Remove the cores from the fruit, slice into rings, and toss with olive oil, salt, and pepper. Grill over a hot fire for 1 minute on each side.

Melon

Halve the melon, spoon out and discard the seeds, then scoop out the flesh in balls. Top with chopped fresh mint.

Fish & Shellfish

The heavily weighted seafood selection at César reflects not only our own predilection toward the sea, but also the prevalence of fish and shellfish dishes on a typical tapas menu in Spain. The coastal areas of the Iberian Peninsula have an embarrassment of seafood riches and, fortunately for us, the West Coast does, too. Throughout the Atlantic and Mediterranean coasts of Spain and Portugal, seafood is eaten with a passion—grilled, fried, poached, sautéed, or oven roasted—and appears in abundance even in landlocked tapas bars, while heavier meat dishes are usually reserved for main meals. To that end, here are some seafood tapas that are standouts at César.

Piquillo Peppers Stuffed with Shrimp and Saffron Alioli

Tigres Rabiosos

Mussels Escabèche

Portuguese-Style Fish Stew

Salt Cod and Potato Cazuela

Salpicón

Squid Stuffed with Caramelized Onions and Bacon

Fried Squid

Croquetas Made with Fish or Shellfish

Grilled Fish with Romesco

Gambas a la Gallega

Piquillo Peppers
Stuffed with Shrimp and Saffron Alioli

Piquillo *peppers are one of the glories of Spanish cuisine, at once sweet and spicy and redolent of the wood fire over which they are roasted. They are also well suited to stuffing, either with cheese, vegetables, or, as in this case, with shrimp. This recipe makes a good amount for a party, and you can easily increase it and reuse the same poaching liquid for additional batches of shrimp.*

To cook the shrimp, wrap the thyme, garlic, chile flakes, pepper-corns, and bay leaf in cheesecloth and tie with string. In a large pot, bring the water, salt, and the bundle of aromatics to a rolling boil. Add half of the shrimp and cook until they are just opaque, about 30 seconds. Drain the shrimp and spread them on a sheet pan to cool. Repeat with the remaining shrimp.

To make the Saffron Alioli, heat the vinegar and saffron in a small nonreactive saucepan over medium heat until hot. Remove from the heat and let stand until cool. Fold the cooled saffron mixture into the Alioli, then fold in the chives, tarragon, cayenne, and lemon zest.

To assemble, roughly chop the shrimp, place in a medium bowl, and fold in ⅔ cup of the Saffron Alioli. Stuff each pepper with about 2 tablespoons of the shrimp mixture. Serve with the remaining Saffron Alioli on each plate and garnish with chives.

MAKES 24 STUFFED PEPPERS

Shrimp

10 sprigs **thyme**

4 or 5 cloves **garlic**, crushed

1 tablespoon **dried red chile flakes**

1 teaspoon **black peppercorns**

1 **bay leaf**

4 quarts **water**

¾ cup **salt**

1 pound small **white shrimp**, peeled

Saffron Alioli

3 tablespoons **white wine vinegar**

¼ teaspoon finely chopped **saffron threads**

1½ cups **Alioli** (page 195)

1 bunch **chives**, finely chopped

2 tablespoons finely chopped fresh **tarragon**

Pinch of **cayenne pepper**

Grated **zest of 2 lemons**

24 **piquillo peppers** (see page 87)

1 bunch **chives**, finely chopped, for garnish

Tigres Rabiosos

*Americans visiting Spain for the first time often mistakenly think that the food will be hot and spicy, like Mexican cuisine. But, in fact, Spanish food, although very full flavored, is relatively mild. This spicy mussel stew is one of the exceptions and is spicy indeed (*tigres *means "tigers" and* rabioso *means "rabid" or "violent" or, in the case of food, "hot"). You can increase the piquancy by adding more chile flakes, but beware: it's easier to increase the heat later than to scale it back once you've finished cooking.*

SERVES 8

Sauce

¼ cup **extra virgin olive oil**

1 **yellow onion**, cut into a thin julienne

2 cloves **garlic**, thinly sliced

1 teaspoon **dried red chile flakes**

4 cups canned diced **tomatoes**, drained

1 teaspoon **salt**

¼ teaspoon freshly ground **black pepper**

Grated **zest of 1 lemon**

Mussels

2 pounds **black mussels** (about 3 dozen), scrubbed

½ cup **dry white wine**

2 cloves **garlic**, crushed

4 sprigs **thyme**

1 **bay leaf**

A few **black peppercorns**

2 tablespoons thinly sliced **fresh chives**

Rock salt, for lining platter

½ **lemon**, for garnish

To make the sauce, heat the oil in a nonreactive 2-quart saucepan over medium heat. Add the onion and cook until translucent, about 10 minutes. Add the garlic and cook until lightly browned, 5 more minutes. Add the chile flakes and tomatoes, turn down the heat to low, and simmer for 30 minutes. Add the salt and pepper. Remove from the heat, purée in a food processor, and, if you want a smoother sauce, run the purée through the small-holed plate of a food mill. Add the lemon zest, return the purée to the saucepan, and set aside.

To cook the mussels, combine them with the wine, garlic, thyme, bay leaf, and peppercorns in a large nonreactive pot with a tight-fitting lid. Bring to a boil over medium heat, cover, and cook until all the mussels have opened, about 5 minutes. Remove from the heat and discard any mussels that have not opened. When they are cool enough to handle, separate the mussels from their shells, discarding half of each shell. Put the mussels in the tomato sauce, add the chives, and reheat gently, just until hot.

To serve, line a platter with the rock salt and arrange the empty shells on top. Spoon a mussel and an ample amount of sauce into each shell. Serve immediately, garnished with the lemon half.

Carrot and Onion Pickle

3 sprigs **thyme**

1 teaspoon **black peppercorns**

1 **bay leaf**

5 **carrots**, peeled, cut lengthwise, and sliced ⅛ inch thick on the diagonal

2 **yellow onions**, cut into thick julienne

2 **jalapeño chiles**, halved lengthwise and stems removed

½ cup **sugar**

2 tablespoons **salt**

¼ cup **sherry vinegar**

2 cups **distilled white vinegar**

4 cups **water**

1 tablespoon **dried red chile flakes**

Mussels

2 pounds **black mussels** (about 3 dozen), scrubbed

½ cup **dry white wine**

4 cloves **garlic**, 2 crushed and 2 thinly sliced

4 sprigs **thyme**

1 **bay leaf**

1 teaspoon **black peppercorns**

¼ cup **extra virgin olive oil**

½ cup **piquillo peppers** (see page 87), cut into a ¼-inch julienne

1 **potato**, peeled, diced, cooked in salted water, and drained

1 **jalapeño chile**, cut in half lengthwise, thinly sliced into half-moons

Mussels Escabèche

The commonly held belief that mussels are an aphrodisiac is only one good reason to enjoy this delicious seafood dish (eat it with someone you love). Escabèche is a pickled dish, versions of which are seen in recipes throughout the Mediterranean region. Some speculate that it may be an ancestor of the wonderful ceviches of South America. This is a great tapa for entertaining because it can be made up to a day ahead of time and served cold. The key to this recipe lies in the carrot pickle; it is a wonderfully tart and spicy condiment that also makes a good accompaniment to all sorts of sandwiches, omelets, and salads. The pickle will keep for up to a month in an airtight container in the refrigerator.

To make the pickle, wrap the thyme, peppercorns, and bay leaf in cheesecloth and tie with string. In a large nonreactive pot, combine the cheesecloth bundle, carrots, onions, jalapeños, sugar, salt, sherry vinegar, distilled vinegar, and water. Bring to a boil, then turn down to a simmer and cook until the carrots and onions are tender, about 15 minutes. Remove from the heat and take out the cheesecloth bundle and discard. Add the chile flakes to the vegetables and chill.

To cook the mussels, combine them with the wine, crushed garlic, thyme, bay leaf, and peppercorns in a large nonreactive pot with a tight-fitting lid. Bring to a boil over medium heat, cover, and cook until all the mussels have opened, about 5 minutes. Remove from the heat and discard any mussels that have not opened. Set aside to cool in the broth.

Heat the oil in a small sauté pan over medium-high heat. Add the sliced garlic and fry until light brown, 2 to 3 minutes. When the mussels are just cool enough to handle, remove them from their shells and discard the shells. Return the mussels to the broth and add the peppers, potato, chile, 1 cup of the pickle, ¾ cup of the pickling juice, and the fried garlic. Chill until ready to serve.

Portuguese-Style Fish Stew

This thick, tomatoey fish stew recalls similar fisherman's stews found on both sides of the Atlantic. Hearty and satisfying, these dishes commonly sustain the fearless men and women who survive by extracting food from the cold, treacherous ocean waters. You can stretch this recipe to feed a few more people simply by adding more seafood; it's a good dish to serve for a dinner party because the sauce and croutons can be made a day in advance. When you sit down to eat, hoist a glass to intrepid fisherfolk everywhere.

To make the sauce, heat the oil in a large nonreactive pot over medium heat. Add the onions and cook, stirring occasionally, until translucent, about 10 minutes. Increase the heat to medium-high, add the garlic, and cook until lightly browned, another 10 minutes. Add the celery and cook for 5 minutes. Add the carrots and cook until they begin to soften, about 10 minutes. Add the peppers, tomatoes, and water and simmer, stirring frequently, until the mixture concentrates, about 45 minutes. Stir in the zest, salt, and pepper.

To assemble the stew, increase the heat to high and add the mussels, clams, and fish pieces. Cover and cook until the shellfish have opened, 2 or 3 minutes. Add the mint and basil and adjust the seasoning. Remove from the heat and discard any shellfish that have not opened.

To serve, place a crouton slice in the bottom of each bowl and ladle the stew over the top.

SERVES 8

Sauce

½ cup **extra virgin olive oil**

3 **yellow onions**, diced

4 teaspoons finely chopped **garlic**

6 tablespoons finely diced **celery**

2 large **carrots**, peeled and grated

⅓ cup finely chopped **piquillo peppers** (see page 87)

4 cups canned diced **tomatoes**, with liquid

1⅓ cups **water**

Grated **zest of 1 orange**

1 tablespoon **salt**

1 teaspoon freshly ground **black pepper**

16 to 20 **black mussels** (about 1 pound), scrubbed

16 to 20 **clams** (about 1 pound), scrubbed

1 pound **grouper** or **sea bass fillet**, cut into bite-sized pieces

¼ cup finely chopped fresh **mint**

¼ cup finely chopped fresh **basil**

Salt and freshly ground **black pepper**

8 sliced **Fried Croutons** (page 202)

Salt Cod and Potato Cazuela

SERVES 8

1 pound **salt cod fillet**, soaked in water for 2 days and water changed daily

1⅓ cups **milk**

1⅓ cups **water**

1 **bay leaf**

4 cloves **garlic**, cut in half

4 sprigs **thyme**

½ **yellow onion**, coarsely chopped

1 teaspoon **black peppercorns**

3 **russet potatoes**, peeled

Salt

½ cup **olive oil infused with garlic**, or as needed

1 cup **heavy cream**, or as needed

2 teaspoons **dried red chile flakes**

½ cup **bread crumbs** from day-old sweet baguette

16 slices **day-old baguette**, each ¼ inch thick and toasted

Basque fisherman—who were probably fishing for cod off the North American coast before Columbus was born—introduced the idea of dried cod to Europe. Books have been written about the importance of cod to the people of Spain and northern Europe, and ultimately to those of New England and Canada. Originally the fish was heavily salted and dried so that it would survive the trip back across the Atlantic in the centuries before refrigeration. It subsequently became food for inland travelers as well, since it kept indefinitely and was tasty and nutritious. Today, people in Spain eat it simply because they like it. There are versions of this dish in cultures around the Mediterranean, and, despite its uncommon status in America, it is one of the most popular tapas at César.

Drain the cod and place it in a large sauté pan. Cover with the milk and water. Wrap the bay leaf, garlic, thyme, onion, and peppercorns in cheesecloth and tie with string. Drop the bundle into the pan, bring to a simmer over low heat, and simmer for 10 minutes. Drain, discard the bundle, and let the cod cool. Pick through the cod and remove any bones.

Meanwhile, cook the potatoes in boiling salted water until tender. Drain the potatoes and mash them with ¼ cup of the oil and ½ cup of the cream in a large bowl.

Preheat the oven to 350°F. Slowly mix the cooked cod with the remaining ¼ cup oil and ½ cup cream just until flaky. Fold the cod into the mashed potatoes. Taste and add more garlic oil or cream, if necessary. Stir in the chile flakes.

Divide the salt cod mixture among 8 individual *cazuelas* (terra-cotta casseroles) or other small baking dishes, and top evenly with the bread crumbs. Bake until golden brown, about 10 minutes. Stick 2 toasted bread slices into each portion and serve immediately.

Salpicón

A salpicón *is usually defined as a meat salad, but it is also a versatile base for all sorts of meaty seafoods like mussels, clams, or grilled fish. At César, Maggie even serves it with a petit filet steak. This version is tart and spicy, a perfect accompaniment to our poached shrimp, and very pretty when displayed on a platter. The same poaching liquid is used for the Gambas a la Gallega (page 164).*

To make the sauce, combine the *piquillos,* jalapeño to taste, cornichons, capers, onions, vinegar, oil, and salt and pepper to taste, and mix thoroughly. Set aside in the refrigerator to chill until needed.

To poach the shrimp, wrap the thyme, garlic, chile flakes, peppercorns, and bay leaf in cheesecloth and tie with string. Add the bundle to a large stockpot filled with heavily salted water and bring to a rapid boil. Drop in a handful of shrimp at a time so as not to lower the temperature of the water, and cook about 30 seconds if small and about 1 minute if larger. The shrimp should be pink and cooked almost through; they will finish cooking out of the water. Using a long-handled skimmer, scoop out the shrimp and spread them on a sheet pan to cool. Repeat until all the shrimp are cooked.

While the shrimp are cooling, brush each baguette piece with the oil and broil or grill until golden brown, 1 to 2 minutes. Immediately rub each piece with the cut side of the garlic clove.

Toss the shrimp with the sauce. On each individual plate, fan out 3 garlic croutons. Place some of the *salpicón* mixture in the middle, and sprinkle with parsley and grated egg.

SERVES 8

Sauce

2 cups coarsely chopped **piquillo peppers** (see page 87)

1 or 2 **jalapeño chiles**, finely chopped

⅓ cup finely chopped **cornichons**

1 cup **salt-packed capers** (see page 86), finely chopped

2 cups finely diced **yellow onions**

¼ cup **white wine vinegar**

1 cup **extra virgin olive oil**

Salt and freshly ground **black pepper**

Shrimp

10 sprigs **thyme**

1 head **garlic**, cut in half crosswise

1 tablespoon **dried red chile flakes**

1 teaspoon **black peppercorns**

1 **bay leaf**

1 pound small **white shrimp**, peeled

1 **baguette**, cut on the diagonal into ½-inch-thick slices

Extra virgin olive oil, for brushing bread

1 clove **garlic**, cut in half

Chopped fresh **flat-leaf parsley**, for garnish

1 **hard-cooked egg**, grated on the large holes of a grater

Squid
Stuffed with Caramelized Onions and Bacon

SERVES 6

Squid

8 ounces **bacon**, cut into ¼-inch dice

3 **yellow onions**, finely diced

¼ cup **heavy cream**

Salt and freshly ground **black pepper**

12 **squid** (about 1 pound), cleaned (see page 203)

Parsley Picada

½ cup **blanched almonds**

1 bunch **flat-leaf parsley**, stems removed

2 cloves **garlic**

1 cup **extra virgin olive oil**

¼ cup freshly squeezed **lemon juice**

Extra virgin olive oil, for coating squid

Salt and freshly ground **black pepper**

Squid is one of the great culinary stars from the sea, but many home cooks are intimidated by the prospect of preparing it. The structure of a squid is actually quite simple, and although it is often sliced into rings and then battered and fried, its unique form cries out for stuffing. Calamares relleños, *or "stuffed squid," are popular fare in tapas bars throughout Spain, with the stuffing ingredients varying regionally. Squid can be filled with almost anything: chopped meats, seafood, rice, vegetables, or even the rest of the squid. Our recipe is based on one Maggie learned at a tapas bar called La Cuchara in San Sebastián. Allowing the onions to caramelize adds richness, while a thinner version of the parsley* picada *we normally use on our* bocadillos *delivers color and acidity to this scrumptious tapa.*

To make the stuffing, sauté the bacon over medium heat in a sauté pan until crisp and most of the fat has been rendered out, about 3 minutes. Using a slotted spoon, transfer the bacon to paper towels to drain. Add the onions to the bacon fat and cook over medium heat, stirring frequently, until caramelized, about 30 minutes. Add the cream, season with salt and pepper, and cook until reduced by half, about 5 minutes. Drain through a sieve, then combine the onions and bacon in a small bowl and mix well. Cover and refrigerate until chilled, about 30 minutes.

Fill the squid bodies with the chilled stuffing, either by spooning it in, or by using a pastry bag with no tip or a large plain tip as we do. As you fill the squid, secure the top of each one with a toothpick to keep the filling in place during cooking.

To make the *picada*, grind the almonds to a fine powder in a food processor. Add the parsley and garlic and continue grinding to a paste. With the machine running, slowly add the oil and lemon juice until the mixture is emulsified, then continue to process for another 3 minutes.

To cook the squid, prepare a hot grill with a grill basket on top, or preheat a large cast-iron skillet until hot, about 4 minutes. Lightly oil each stuffed body and all the tentacles, and season with salt and pepper. Place the stuffed bodies and tentacles in the basket or skillet and cook, turning once, until nicely browned, about 2 minutes on each side. Transfer to individual plates, dividing evenly, and remove the toothpicks. Drizzle each serving with the *picada* and serve at once.

Fried Squid

Without a doubt, squid cut into rings and fried is the most popular way to serve these little cephalopods in America. They are one of the most perfect cocktail appetizers ever conceived, going well with all sorts of mixed drinks, sherry, and white or rosé wines. They are also easy to fry, providing you get your oil sufficiently hot and don't overcook them. Garbanzo (chickpea) flour can be purchased in most health food and specialty food stores and is sometimes called by its Italian name, ceci *flour. These are also very good with* Alioli *(page 195).*

Cut the bodies of the squid into rings about ¼ inch wide. In a large bowl, combine the water and salt, and add the squid rings and tentacles. Let soak for 20 minutes. Drain and rinse in a colander.

While the squid are soaking, combine the flours, paprika, salt, and pepper in a wide, shallow bowl.

Heat the oil to 375°F in a large, deep pot. Working with a handful of squid at a time, dredge it in the flour mixture, shake off the excess, and place it in the hot oil. Here the process becomes, as Maggie says, "more of a hearing thing than a seeing thing." In other words, when the sizzle from the hot oil dies down, remove the squid with a long-handled skimmer and place on paper towels to drain. They cook very fast, in 15 to 20 seconds, and you don't want to overcook them. Repeat with the remaining squid, keeping the cooked squid in a warm oven.

Divide the squid among individual plates and drizzle with Mojo Picón. Garnish with a few caperberries.

SERVES 6

2 pounds **squid** (about 24 squid), cleaned (see page 203)

4 quarts **water**

½ cup **salt**

1 cup **all-purpose flour**

1 cup **garbanzo (chickpea) flour**

1 cup **semolina flour**

1 tablespoon **paprika**

1 tablespoon **kosher salt**

1 teaspoon freshly ground **black pepper**

8 cups **peanut oil**

Mojo Picón (page 197), for drizzling

Caperberries (see page 86), for garnish

Croquetas
Made with Fish or Shellfish

MAKES 24 CROQUETAS

2 cups finely flaked **cooked fish fillet** (such as halibut, sea bass, or salmon) or finely chopped cooked lobster, clam, or shrimp meat

6 cups **bread crumbs** from a day-old sweet baguette

2 **eggs**

1 **jalapeño chile**, finely chopped

2 cups thinly sliced **scallion**, white part only

1 bunch **cilantro**, stems removed and finely chopped

1½ cups diced **piquillo peppers** (see page 87)

Grated **zest** and **juice of 2 lemons**

2 teaspoons **salt**

1 teaspoon freshly ground **black pepper**

½ teaspoon **cayenne pepper**

3 cups **peanut oil**

Alioli (page 195)

Lemon wedges, for garnish

Despite the long list of ingredients, these croquettes are quite simple to make, and they are great for feeding a group of people. This recipe is also a good way to use up leftover fish from the night before. The heat can be adjusted in these, and it is balanced nicely by the sweet peppers and the lemon zest.

In a large bowl, mix together the seafood, bread crumbs, eggs, jalapeño, scallion, cilantro, *piquillo* peppers, lemon zest and juice, salt, black pepper, and cayenne pepper. Form into 24 patties each about 2 inches in diameter and ¼ inch thick.

Heat the oil to 375°F in a large, deep pot. Fry the patties in batches of 4 to 6, turning once, until they are golden brown, about 2 minutes. Using a slotted spoon, transfer to paper towels to drain and keep hot in a warm oven. Serve immediately with the Alioli and lemon wedges.

Grilled Fish
with Romesco

This is an easy and delicious way to cook firm-fleshed fish fillets such as tuna, swordfish, halibut, or salmon. The simple marinade enhances the fish and helps keep it moist, whether you are cooking for 8 or 80. This is also good served with our Mojo Verde (page 197) in place of the Romesco Sauce, or you can offer both.

In a large, shallow bowl, mix together the oil, zest, and thyme. Toss the fish in the marinade, cover, and refrigerate for 30 minutes.

Prepare a hot grill. Remove the fish from the marinade, season with salt and pepper, and grill until just cooked through, about 2 minutes on each side. Serve with Romesco Sauce.

SERVES 8

¼ cup **extra virgin olive oil**

Grated **zest of 1 lemon**

½ bunch **thyme**

8 firm-fleshed **fish fillets**
(2½ to 3 ounces each)

Salt and freshly ground **black pepper**

Romesco Sauce (page 196)

Gambas a la Gallega

SERVES 8

10 sprigs **thyme**

1 head **garlic**, cut in half crosswise

1 tablespoon **dried red chile flakes**

1 teaspoon **black peppercorns**

1 **bay leaf**

2 pounds large **shrimp** (32 to 48 shrimp)

Garnish

Extra virgin olive oil

Gallega Spice (page 199)

Salt

Lemon wedges

This is a spicy and colorful way to serve shrimp. The Gallega Spice, a mixture of different ground peppers, is our version of a common seafood seasoning used in Galicia, especially for shrimp and octopus. You can leave the shrimp in their shells (the way you would probably find them in Spain), or you can shell them, making it a bit easier on your guests. Either way, the shrimp should be served immediately after they are cooked and seasoned. A shaker can for dispensing the spice mix is a handy tool for this recipe.

Wrap the thyme, garlic, chile flakes, peppercorns, and bay leaf in cheesecloth and tie with string. Add the bundle to a large stockpot filled with heavily salted water and bring to a rapid boil. Drop in a handful of shrimp at a time so as not to lower the temperature of the water, and cook for 2 to 3 minutes. The shrimp should be pink and cooked almost through; they will finish cooking out of the water. Using a long-handled skimmer, scoop out the shrimp and spread them on a sheet pan to cool briefly. Repeat until all the shrimp are cooked.

When the shrimp are cool enough to handle, distribute them evenly among individual plates. Drizzle with the oil and dust with Gallega Spice and salt. Serve immediately with lemon wedges.

Bocadillos

Bocadillos are the sandwiches found in nearly every tapas bar and café in Spain, and they are a popular component of the César menu. Literally "little bites" or "mouthfuls," they are typically not considered meals, but rather something to tide you over until it's time for a meal. In Spain, they are eaten mostly standing up as a quick lunch or even a late breakfast. At their most basic and most common, they are simply a baguette with thin slices of *jamón serrano*, or sometimes slices of tortilla (Spanish omelet). However, as shown here, *bocadillos* come with a variety of cooked fillings that elevate them from a snack to a meal. The instructions call for ten-inch-long sandwiches, but they can just as easily be cut into smaller pieces for a party. The smaller siblings to *bocadillos* are called *montaditos,* which literally means "little mounds." Again, these can be made up with anything from a slice of ham or other pork product to cheese to deep-fried fish. We present two versions here that make excellent use of the famed anchovies of Spain.

Escalivada

Pork Loin Bocadillo

Spicy Tuna Salad

Manchego and Greens

Montaditos with Boquerones and Olive Relish

Montaditos with Boquerones and Alioli

Pan y Tomate

Escalivada

MAKES 6 TO 8 SANDWICHES

Eggplant

2 **eggplants**, tops and bottoms trimmed, and cut lengthwise into 8 wedges each

1 tablespoon **salt**

1 teaspoon freshly ground **black pepper**

½ cup **extra virgin olive oil**

Anchovy Paste

½ cup **anchovies** packed in olive oil

2 cloves **garlic**

⅛ teaspoon **dried red chile flakes**

⅛ teaspoon freshly ground **black pepper**

2 tablespoons **extra virgin olive oil**

1 tablespoon **sherry vinegar**

3 or 4 **baguettes**

1 clove **garlic**, cut in half

20 **piquillo peppers** (see page 87), halved to lie flat

1 bunch **flat-leaf parsley**

Maggie discovered this scrumptious sandwich while eating at the Cervecería Catalan in Barcelona. The anchovy paste (essentially the base for a Caesar salad dressing) can be applied according to your taste, but it should not overpower the slightly caramelized eggplant. You can also serve the filling as a salad of sorts: layer the vegetables, possibly on a bed of greens, and top with the anchovy paste and parsley. Just be sure to provide plenty of bread to scoop up the eggplant.

To roast the eggplant, preheat the oven to 400°F. Line a sheet pan with parchment paper. Toss the eggplants in a large bowl with the with salt, pepper, and oil. Place the wedges skin side down on the sheet pan and roast until they are soft, spongy, and have a rich, roasted color, about 40 minutes. Remove from the oven and, when cool enough to handle, remove the skin from the eggplants. Tear the meat into thin strips. Set aside.

To make the Anchovy Paste, combine the anchovies, garlic, chile flakes, and pepper in a food processor and process to a smooth paste. With the machine running, slowly add the oil and vinegar until the mixture emulsifies.

To assemble, cut the baguettes into 10-inch lengths, and then slice them in half lengthwise, leaving a hinge. Rub the inside of the bread with the cut side of the garlic. Spread with the Anchovy Paste. Layer a few eggplant strips and 6 *piquillo* halves per sandwich, and top with parsley leaves.

Pork Loin Bocadillo

Our recipe for roasted pork loin makes a great meal in itself, and you can save the leftovers for this delicious sandwich, or make it just for this reason. The brining process, adapted from a recipe by chef Todd English of Olives restaurant, renders a juicy and delicious pork loin. You'll need to start the brining at least 2 days in advance.

To brine the pork, combine the water, garlic, onion, honey, salt, bay leaf, mustard seed, nutmeg, peppercorns, chile flakes, and rosemary in a large saucepan over medium-high heat, and heat to dissolve the honey and infuse the spices. Place the ice in a large glass bowl. Pour the honey mixture over the ice. When the ice has melted, add the pork. Cover and cure in the refrigerator for 2 days.

To roast the pork, preheat the oven to 425°F. Mix together the oil and Moruño Spice in a small bowl. Remove the pork from the brine and discard the brine. Pat the meat dry and rub it all over with ¼ cup of the oil-and-spice mixture. Preheat a cast-iron skillet over medium-high heat for 5 minutes. Sear the meat for about 2 minutes on each side. Transfer to the oven and roast until the internal temperature is 135°F, about 30 minutes. Remove the loin from the pan and let it rest for 20 minutes, then slice into thin medallions.

To assemble, cut the baguettes into 10-inch lengths, and then slice them in half lengthwise, leaving a hinge. Rub the inside of the bread with the cut side of the garlic. Spread the Alioli over the bread. Layer the pork medallions on the bread, drizzle with the remaining oil-and-spice mixture, sprinkle with salt, and top with arugula leaves.

MAKES 6 TO 8 SANDWICHES

Brine

3 cups **water**

1 head **garlic**, cut in half crosswise

1 **yellow onion**, coarsely chopped

2½ cups **honey**

2 tablespoons **salt**

1 **bay leaf**

2 tablespoons **mustard seed**

Pinch of freshly ground **nutmeg**

2 tablespoons **black peppercorns**

2 tablespoons **dried red chile flakes**

1 bunch **rosemary**, cut into 1-inch lengths

6 cups **ice**

1 center-cut **pork loin** (about 4 pounds)

½ cup **extra virgin olive oil**

3 tablespoons **Moruño Spice** (page 199)

3 or 4 **baguettes**

2 or 3 cloves **garlic**, cut in half

Alioli (page 195)

Salt

2 cups loosely packed **arugula leaves**

Spicy Tuna Salad

MAKES 6 TO 8 SANDWICHES

Hard-Boiled Eggs

8 cups **water**

1 teaspoon **distilled white vinegar**

Pinch of **salt**

6 **eggs**

Tuna Salad

12 ounces (two 6-ounce cans) **tuna in oil**

20 **green olives**, pitted and finely chopped

2 **scallions**, white and green parts, chopped

⅔ cup **salt-packed capers** (see page 86), rinsed and coarsely chopped

⅓ cup finely chopped fresh **flat-leaf parsley**

1 **jalapeño chile**, minced

1 ½ cups **extra virgin olive oil**

2 teaspoons **dried red chile flakes**

Juice of 3 **lemons**

3 or 4 **baguettes**

Salt

2 cups loosely packed **arugula leaves**

This is probably not the tuna salad your mother used to make. But then again, you're all grown up now, and perhaps you have discovered that tuna is not really a chicken of the sea but, in the right hands, a delicious and versatile fish. Be sure to use the best-quality tuna you can find (at César we use an imported Spanish tuna that is packed in olive oil). Our tuna salad has just enough heat from the chiles and plenty of zest from the capers. The method we use to make hard-boiled eggs results in slightly soft yolks that won't have a gray ring. We serve this salad in a bocadillo, *but it is also a great choice for stuffing tomatoes or* piquillo *peppers (see page 87), spreading on* crostini, *or serving on a bed of fresh greens.*

To cook the eggs, combine the water, vinegar, and salt in a nonreactive saucepan and bring to a rapid boil. Gently place the eggs into the water and set a timer for 9 minutes. Meanwhile, prepare a bowl of ice water. When the timer goes off, remove the eggs immediately and drop them into the ice water to stop the cooking. Let them chill in the ice water for at least 20 minutes before you peel them. If cooked and peeled ahead of time, store the eggs in cold water until needed.

To make the salad, open the tuna and discard the top layer of oil. Do not rinse the tuna. Place the tuna in a large bowl and add the olives, scallions, capers, parsley, jalapeño, oil, chile flakes, and lemon juice. Fold together gently. Do not break apart the tuna too much; there should be a nice mix of small and large pieces.

To assemble, cut the baguettes into 10-inch lengths, and then slice them in half lengthwise, leaving a hinge. Spread the tuna mixture over the bread. Slice the hard-cooked eggs crosswise ⅛ inch thick and layer them on top. Sprinkle with salt and top with arugula leaves.

Manchego and Greens

Manchego is the cheese that put Spanish cheese making on the map. It is a firm, nutty sheep's milk cheese and hails from the same windswept plains of La Mancha that Don Quixote traveled, hence the name (manchego means "of La Mancha"). It is the best-known Spanish cheese, even inside Spain, and is featured in nearly every tapas bar in the land, usually cut into thin wedges and marinated in extra virgin olive oil. Delicious as a simple snacking cheese, it also shines as the base for this bocadillo. Manchego is available in varying ages, from about three months old to over two years; we like to use a young cheese for this sandwich.

To prepare the greens, heat the oil in a large, deep pan over medium heat. Add the garlic and cook until it is opaque, about 10 seconds. Throw in the chile flakes, and cook just until they begin to bleed into the oil, about 5 seconds. Throw in the arugula and cook, turning and tossing with tongs, until it is completely wilted, about 1 minute. Remove to a colander and season with salt.

To assemble, cut the baguettes into 10-inch lengths, and then slice them in half lengthwise, leaving a hinge. Rub the inside of the bread with the cut side of the garlic. Cover with the greens and squeeze a few drops of lemon juice over the top. Add a layer of cheese and drizzle with the Herb Oil.

MAKES 6 TO 8 SANDWICHES

Greens

2 tablespoons **extra virgin olive oil**

2 cloves **garlic**, crushed

½ teaspoon **dried red chile flakes**

2 bunches **arugula**, tough stems removed

Salt

3 or 4 **baguettes**

2 or 3 cloves **garlic**, cut in half

Juice of 1 **lemon**

24 thin slices **Manchego cheese**

Herb Oil (page 198)

Olive Relish

1½ cups **picholine olives**, pitted and coarsely chopped

¾ teaspoon finely chopped **salt-packed capers** (see page 86)

¼ teaspoon **dried red chile flakes**

½ teaspoon finely chopped **garlic**

¼ cup finely chopped fresh **flat-leaf parsley**

Grated **zest** and **juice of 1 orange**

¼ cup **extra virgin olive oil**

½ teaspoon freshly ground **black pepper**

1 **baguette**

1 bunch **flat-leaf parsley**

Boquerones (see page 86)

SERVES 6 TO 8

Spicy Green Olives

3 cloves **garlic**

1 teaspoon **salt**

2 cups **picholine olives** or other good green olives

2 tablespoons **extra virgin olive oil**

2 tablespoons **Moruño Spice** (page 199)

1 **baguette**

Alioli (page 195)

Boquerones (see page 86)

Montaditos
with Boquerones and Olive Relish

Boquerones *are tender white anchovies from the Cantabrian coast in northern Spain, usually packed in vinegar and olive oil. Like much of the canned fish and seafood of Spain, they are legendary, and it is well worth the effort to get them, either by mail order or at a local specialty shop (see Resources). Here are two ways we serve these delicious and unique anchovies, both very simple and great for cocktail parties. We also serve them on top of our Pan y Tomate (page 176). The olive relish keeps well in an airtight container in the refrigerator.*

To make the relish, thoroughly mix together all of the ingredients in a medium bowl.

To assemble, cut the baguette on the diagonal into ¼-inch-thick slices. Spread each slice with the relish, then top with a few leaves of parsley and an anchovy fillet.

Montaditos
with Boquerones and Alioli

To make the olives, put the garlic and salt in a mortar and pound to a paste. In a medium bowl, mix together the garlic paste, olives, oil, and spice mix, and let stand for 2 hours.

To assemble, cut the baguette on the diagonal into ¼-inch-thick slices. Spread each slice with Alioli and top with an anchovy fillet. Serve with the spiced olives.

Pan y Tomate

SERVES 6 TO 8

1 large loaf **crusty white bread**, cut into ½-inch-thick slices

Extra virgin olive oil, for brushing bread

2 or 3 cloves **garlic**, cut in half

Several ripe **tomatoes**, cut in half

Thin slices **jamón serrano**
(see page 88; optional)

Boquerones (see page 86; optional)

This simple tomato bread, known in Catalan as pa amb tomàquet, *can serve as the base for any number of toppings or can be eaten by itself. Its presence is pervasive throughout Catalonia, sometimes with garlic, sometimes without, but always with ripe, in-season tomatoes and the excellent, cold-pressed olive oil of the region. We prefer to grill ours lightly before dressing it, which also helps release the flavor of the garlic.*

Prepare a hot grill. Lightly brush one side of the bread slices with oil and grill on both sides until they are golden brown but not burnt, about 15 seconds on each side. Immediately rub the oiled side of each slice with the cut side of a garlic clove and then with the cut side of a tomato. Serve as is, or top with either a slice of *jámon serrano* or an anchovy.

Spanish Cheese, El país de 100 quesos

(the land of 100 cheeses)

When Don Quixote, in the famous chronicles of his adventures, said, "While I am eating, I know nothing. But when I have finished eating, I begin to understand," it is very likely that what he was eating—and understanding—was cheese. Perhaps no other product so typifies Spain's adherence to traditional foods and methods of production as this most ancient of foods. Some of the most exciting cheeses coming from Europe these days are from Spain, home to more than 100 distinct cheeses made in every region of the country, fashioned from all three major milk types: cow, sheep, and goat. Spain is challenging its other cheese-famous neighbors to the north and east in terms of quality, quantity, and originality, and they have been doing it since at least the time of the Romans, who nurtured the craft of cheese making wherever they went. Spain was among the first European nations to establish a Denomination of Origin (DO) certification for its cheeses, a system derived from the world of wine and now extended to foods other than cheese, such as olive oil, rice, seafood products, and produce.

In Spain, cheese is not eaten as dessert, as it is in France, or used extensively in cooking, as it so often is in Italy. But it is part of everyday life, eaten for breakfast, lunch, and as tapas in the evening. (The exception is the creamy, sweet *mel i mato* from Catalonia, a lovely light dessert that could also serve as an afternoon snack; see page 190.) At César, we serve a cheese plate made up of several slices of different cheeses accompanied by *membrillo*, a succulent quince paste that is made and enjoyed throughout Spain. You won't find many cheese-based dishes in the recipe section because there aren't many in the Spanish repertoire. It would be rare indeed, however, to walk into a tapas bar in Spain and not find a selection of cheeses to be enjoyed with a glass of sherry or a cold beer.

One could easily draw lines on the map delineating the preferred type of dairy animal in each region. Sheep rule on the vast central plains, watched over by the giant Osborne-bull billboards that dot the countryside—huge black silhouettes that advertise the famous sherry and brandy producer. In fact, La Mancha's prolific ewes produce most of the milk used for making cheese in Spain, including the famous Manchego (see page 173). Other great ewe's milk cheeses include Roncal from Navarre, the buttery, rich semihard cheese that was the first cheese in Spain to be awarded the prestigious DO certification; the longer-aged, slightly more piquant Zamorano from Castile-León; and the unique, full-flavored Idiazábal, a sharp smoked cheese from the Basque country. From Extremadura in the west comes a very different cheese, La Serena, a luscious, buttery, almost molten cheese that at its peak of maturity must be eaten with a spoon.

The Celts who first settled "Green Spain" (as the northern part of the peninsula is aptly called) brought with them their beloved cows, which fared well in the lush, rain-fed, verdant hills and the alpinelike mountain valleys that stretch from Galicia to the Pyrenees. It is here, in the Picos de Europa, that we find the second highest mountains in all of Europe, and several distinctive cow's milk cheeses including tetilla, a mild and pleasant cheese from Galicia that is doubtless noted as much for its resemblance to a breast (the name means "little teat") as for its flavor. Farther over in Asturias, cow's milk goes into the lusty and piquant afuega'l pitu, which translates roughly as "fire in the throat." Not for the faint at heart, this assertive cheese has a strong aroma that is matched by its sharp, almost abrasive flavor. It is Spain's answer to the strong, washed-rind examples from France. Cow's milk also accounts for one of the world's great blues, Cabrales from Asturias, a forthright, intensely flavored cheese that can also include goat's and sheep's milk in the mix. This cheese has the added distinction—at least according to the Spanish—of being the world's first blue. Cows and their milk are also favored in the Mediterranean's Balearic Islands, a holdover from when the British owned the beautiful and lush archipelago. The island of Menorca produces a lovely, pillow-shaped cheese called Mahón. It is a simple, easy-to-like cheese that gains complexity as it ages, taking on Parmesan-like depths of flavor, with its creamy paste turning a bit crumbly and the overall color swooning toward butterscotch.

The eastern coastline of Spain, from Malaga to Barcelona, as well as the Canary Islands off the coast of Morocco, is goat country, home of those hardy, ubiquitous animals that thrive where other animals could not survive. They produce far less milk than either cows or sheep, but their milk provides a distinctive flavor and some wonderful cheeses, such as the great Majorero from the island of Fuerteventura, the easternmost island of the Canary archipelago. Unlike most goat cheeses that Americans are used to, Majorero is a slightly sharp, tangy, firm cheese that is usually rubbed with either olive oil, paprika, or *gofio*, the singular toasted corn-meal so favored by the people of the islands. Back on the mainland, Extremadura produces the buttery, melt-in-your-mouth Ibores, a firm goat cheese that is rubbed with oil or paprika. Other goat cheeses include Murcia al vino, also known as "drunken goat," so-called because it is cured in a bath of red wine that not only colors the rind, but also lends a distinctive floral note to the paste; and Garrotxa, the delicious Catalonian goat cheese that bears a lovely grayish blue downy mold.

There are dozens more cheeses—some that are rarely seen beyond their region of origin and others that are making inroads in American markets. Cheeses that were unheard of only a few years ago are showing up in ever-increasing quantities, enhancing our tables and influencing the production of our own cheeses.

Sweets

Spain has a collective sweet tooth, one of the legacies of centuries of Arab occupation. Since America shares this love of sweets, our dessert list has always been popular at César. From the more conventional cookies and puddings to deep-fried *churros* to the Mel i Mato, which is really more about assemblage than cooking, we present a glimpse at the world of Spanish desserts.

In line with the tapas menu, our desserts tend to be tapas-sized confections rather than towering extravaganzas, and you'll find no architectural creations here. Sweets at César are generally simple preparations that allow the taste of such ingredients as almonds, the liquorice-flavored anise, and sweetened rice to shine through. Most of these desserts can easily be served as tapas at a party, and some, like *churros,* are great fun to make for a group.

Catalan-Style Cookies

Anise Almond Cookies

Rice Pudding

Churros with Bittersweet Chocolate Sauce

Mel i Mato

Crema de Chocolate

Bread Pudding with Orange Caramel Sauce

Flamenco night at César.

Catalan-Style Cookies

These are called panellets *in Spain, meaning "little breads." They are traditionally served on All Saints' Day, usually in a whole range of flavors. In past centuries, most people throughout Europe didn't celebrate their birthday (it was considered rude to congratulate a lady on her birthday), but rather their saint's day, the day devoted to the saint for whom they were named. If the person did not have the name of a saint, then he or she celebrated the day of all saints, hence the holiday and the occasion for this cookie.*

To cook the sweet potatoes, preheat the oven to 350°F. Roast the sweet potatoes until soft, about 1 hour. Remove from the oven and let cool. Remove and discard the skins from the sweet potatoes and measure 1 cup cooked potato.

Toss the almonds with the coconut and set aside. In a food processor, combine the cooked sweet potato, 2 cups of the sugar, the egg yolks, vanilla, and lemon zest, and process until well mixed. Transfer to a large bowl and mix in the almonds and coconut. Let the dough rest, covered, for at least 30 minutes in the refrigerator.

Preheat the oven to 350°F. Line 2 sheet pans with parchment paper. Place the remaining 1 cup sugar in a small bowl. Form the cookie dough into perfectly round balls about 1 inch in diameter. Roll the balls in the sugar, then place 1 inch apart on the sheet pans.

Bake until the cookies start to crack on top, about 15 minutes. Transfer to racks and let cool completely before serving.

MAKES ABOUT 48 COOKIES

1 large or 2 small **sweet potatoes** (about ¾ pound)

3 cups **blanched almonds**, finely ground

2 cups **shredded coconut**

3 cups **sugar**

2 **egg yolks**

1 teaspoon **vanilla extract**

Grated **zest of 1 lemon**

Anise Almond Cookies

MAKES ABOUT 24 COOKIES

1 cup **all-purpose flour**

¾ cup **blanched almonds**, finely ground

½ cup **granulated sugar**

Pinch of **salt**

½ teaspoon **ground cinnamon**

1 tablespoon **anise seed**

1 **egg**

½ cup **vegetable shortening** or **lard**

¼ cup **confectioners' sugar**

These traditional cookies are typically made with lard, but you can get almost the same consistency with vegetable shortening.

Toast the flour in a dry, heavy-bottomed skillet over low heat for 5 minutes, stirring frequently so as not to let it brown. The flour should pick up a nutty flavor. Sift the flour into a large bowl. Add the ground almonds, granulated sugar, salt, cinnamon, and anise seed, and toss to mix well. In a small bowl, lightly whisk the egg. Add the egg and shortening to the flour mixture and mix well with your hands or a wooden spoon.

Preheat the oven to 300°F. Line 2 sheet pans with parchment paper. Using a #60 (1-ounce) ice-cream scoop, scoop out the dough and roll it into balls 1 inch in diameter. Place the balls 1 inch apart on the sheet pans. Press each cookie lightly with your thumb, just enough to make a small dimple. Bake until the cookies are golden brown, about 30 minutes. Transfer to racks and let cool completely, then dust with the confectioners' sugar.

Rice Pudding

SERVES 6

1¾ cups **whole milk**

1 **cinnamon stick**

Zest of 1 lemon

¼ cup **short-grain rice**

¾ cup **sugar**

2 tablespoons **unsalted butter**

2 tablespoons **anise liqueur** such as Ricard or Pernod

This rice pudding combines the creaminess of a traditional rice pudding with the burnt sugar crust of a crème brûlée.

In a large saucepan, heat the milk, cinnamon stick, and zest over low heat. When hot, add the rice and cook over low heat for 40 minutes, stirring frequently with a wooden spoon. Turn up the heat to medium and simmer until all the rice has puffed up and the milk has thickened, about 10 more minutes. Keep a close watch at this stage, and stir often. Add ½ cup of the sugar and the butter and cook for another 10 minutes. Add the liqueur, stir to incorporate, and divide among six 6-ounce ramekins. Let cool, cover, and refrigerate until well chilled, or for up to 24 hours.

Just before serving, sprinkle the tops evenly with the remaining $\frac{1}{4}$ cup sugar. Slip under a preheated broiler until the sugar caramelizes into a nice, even golden brown, or caramelize with a kitchen torch. Serve immediately.

Churros
with Bittersweet Chocolate Sauce

MAKES ABOUT 8 CHURROS

Chocolate Sauce

10 ounces **semisweet chocolate chips** or bulk semisweet chocolate chopped into bits

½ cup **honey**

2 cups **half-and-half**

6 tablespoons **Dutch-process cocoa**

Churros

3 tablespoons **unsalted butter**

1 teaspoon **sugar**

Pinch of **salt**

Grated **zest of 1 orange**

Grated **zest of 1 lemon**

1 cup **water**

1 ½ cups **all-purpose flour**, sifted

2 **eggs**

3 cups **peanut oil**

1 cup **sugar**, for coating

1 tablespoon ground **cinnamon**, for coating

For anyone who has experienced the obligatory Madrid early morning ritual of dipping freshly fried churros *in thick, hot chocolate, the taste memory will live forever, especially if it came on the tail end of a proper night out among the Madrileños. It is a remarkably sensual experience. The long, slender, spiraling* churros *(or their thicker cousins,* porras*) exist solely for dunking into chocolate, although they can also be dusted with confectioners' sugar. In Spain, a special* churro *press is used to extrude the batter (see Resources), but you can use a cookie press or a pastry bag. The Spanish love their chocolate—it was there, after all, that chocolate made its European debut—so much so that a special dispensation from the Pope allows them to consume it on fast days. Breakfast and the cold, gray light of dawn aside, our version of* churros *and chocolate sauce also makes a lovely dessert or teatime snack.*

To make the sauce, place the chocolate into a large heatproof bowl and set aside. Heat the honey and half-and-half to a near simmer over medium heat in a small, heavy-bottomed saucepan. Remove from the heat and whisk in the cocoa. Immediately strain the milk mixture through a fine sieve into the bowl of chocolate, pushing through any cocoa lumps with a rubber spatula and scraping the sieve clean. Whisk the milk mixture to melt the chocolate. You should have a smooth sauce with the consistency of a light cream soup. Keep it warm over a double boiler while you make the *churros*.

To make the *churros*, combine the butter, sugar, salt, orange and lemon zests, and water in a large saucepan, and bring to a full boil, stirring constantly. Once the butter has melted, beat in the flour all at once and continue to cook for another 30 seconds. Transfer the dough to a stand mixer fitted with a paddle attachment and beat in the eggs, one at a time, on medium-high speed. Continue to mix for several minutes, or until the dough forms soft peaks.

In a large, deep pot, heat the oil to 375°F. Sift together the sugar and cinnamon into a wide, shallow dish and set aside. Transfer the dough to a pastry bag fitted with a large star tip, or fill a *churro* press. Pipe the dough into the oil, forming a spiral about 12 inches long. When it is golden brown on one side, after about 30 seconds, flip it over with a pair of tongs and finish cooking, about 20 seconds longer. Remove from the oil and drain briefly on paper towels, then dredge both sides in the cinnamon sugar. Repeat with the remaining dough, holding the finished *churros* in a warm oven. Serve immediately with the bittersweet chocolate sauce.

Mel i Mato

Fromage blanc or other **soft, fresh cheese**

Toasted almonds

Fresh fruit, such as nectarines, figs, oranges, clementines, blood oranges, or strawberries; or **dried fruit,** such as figs, apricots, or strawberries

Wildflower Honey

Many cheese makers in Spain, whether they make hard or soft cheese, like to consume their freshly made cheese as a dessert with honey poured over it. In Catalonia, the tradition has evolved into a very specific dish called mel i mato, *or "honey and cheese," served with all manner of nuts or fruits, depending on what's in season. The cheese they use is a fresh curd cheese made from the region's fine goat's milk. At César, we use a wonderful fromage blanc, a fresh, simple cheese made locally by the Cowgirl Creamery. In a pinch, you can use a fresh goat cheese. Whatever cheese you choose, it should be very soft and have a fresh, milky taste. Be sure to choose a good-quality wildflower honey to accompany it. This is one of the most often-requested desserts at César, and is not so much a recipe as it is a list of suggestions and instructions for assembly.*

Place the cheese in the middle of the plate. Strew various fruits and nuts around the plate, and drizzle honey over the top.

Crema de Chocolate

This is a velvety smooth, deliciously decadent way to end a meal or simply to indulge yourself. Just knowing that these are in the refrigerator could get you through a bad day. Use the best-quality chocolate you can get. We recommend Valrhona 70 percent cacao. For the liqueur, we use Gran Torres, a relatively inexpensive but good-quality Spanish orange liqueur, but you can use Cointreau, Grand Marnier, or even good triple sec.

Combine the chocolate, liqueur, and vanilla in a large heatproof bowl and set aside.

Combine the egg yolks and 1 tablespoon of the sugar in a medium bowl and whisk until blended. Set aside.

Heat the cream, the remaining 2 tablespoons sugar, the cinnamon, and the orange zest over medium heat in a large saucepan until steam is rising. Do not let the cream boil.

Pour ½ cup of the hot cream mixture into the yolks and whisk together to temper them. Pour the egg mixture into the hot cream mixture. Using a heat-resistant rubber spatula, stir constantly over medium-low heat until the pudding thickens enough to coat the back of a spoon, about 5 minutes.

Pour the pudding over the chocolate and whisk until the chocolate melts and the mixture is blended. Strain the mixture through a fine sieve. Divide among eight 3-ounce ramekins and chill, uncovered, for 2 hours. Wrap with plastic and refrigerate until serving.

To serve, top each portion with a few toasted hazelnuts and a dollop of whipped cream, then dust with cinnamon.

SERVES 8

6 ounces **semisweet chocolate chips** or bulk semisweet chocolate chopped into bits

1 tablespoon **orange liqueur**

1½ teaspoons **vanilla extract**

6 **egg yolks**

3 tablespoons **sugar**

2 cups **heavy cream**

¼ teaspoon **ground cinnamon**

Grated **zest of 1 orange**

Garnish

16 toasted **hazelnuts**, skins removed (see page 196)

½ cup **heavy cream**, whipped

2 tablespoons **ground cinnamon**

Bread Pudding
with Orange Caramel Sauce

SERVES 8

Bread Pudding

4 cups **milk**

1½ cups **granulated sugar**

1 **cinnamon stick**

Grated **zest of 2 oranges**

12 cups **cubed bread** (¼-inch cubes)

6 **egg yolks**

2 **eggs**

Sauce

2 cups freshly squeezed **blood orange juice** or regular **orange juice**

1 cup **heavy cream**

4 tablespoons **unsalted butter**

1 cup **granulated sugar**

Garnish

½ cup **heavy cream**, whipped

¼ cup **confectioners' sugar**

Just about every culture that makes bread has its own version of bread pudding. This one has a decidedly Spanish-Moorish flavor from the orange zest as well as the orange caramel sauce. In Spain, the sauce would invariably be made with blood oranges. They not only have a deep, lovely color, but also an intense flavor. If you can find them, try them; otherwise, seek out the sweetest oranges in the market. This recipe is designed for individual ramekins, but it can easily be adapted for a larger baking dish. You will have to bake it a little longer, testing it for doneness by inserting a knife into the center, as you would a cake; it is done when the knife comes out clean. Note that this recipe needs to be started the night before.

To make the pudding, heat the milk, granulated sugar, cinnamon stick, and orange zest in a medium saucepan over medium heat until the sugar dissolves. Let cool, cover, and refrigerate overnight to steep.

Preheat the oven to 350°F. Put the bread cubes in a large bowl. Reheat the milk mixture and remove the cinnamon stick. In a large bowl, lightly whisk together the yolks and eggs. Pour the milk mixture into the eggs and mix thoroughly. Pour this mixture over the bread and allow to soak for a few minutes.

Butter the insides of eight 5-ounce ramekins. Divide the mixture among the ramekins and place them in a roasting pan or on a large, deep sheet pan. Pour about 1 inch of water into the pan to create a water bath. Bake until a knife inserted in the center comes out clean, about 1¼ hours.

To make the sauce, bring the orange juice to a simmer over medium-high heat in a medium saucepan, and reduce to ¼ cup, about 10 minutes. Strain through a fine sieve into a bowl, add the cream, and set aside. In another saucepan, melt the butter over medium heat. Add the granulated sugar and continue to cook, stirring frequently until the sugar is lightly caramelized, about 3 minutes. Add the orange juice mixture, stirring constantly. Simmer for 5 minutes and strain through a fine sieve.

Serve the pudding warm, either turned out onto individual plates or left inside the ramekins. Top with the sauce, a dollop of whipped cream, and a dusting of confectioners' sugar.

Basics

The recipes in this section are used in dishes throughout the Tapas section of the book. Many of them, such as *alioli*, *romesco*, and some of the spice mixes, are great with all sorts of foods other than tapas. Once you've tasted them you'll find other uses for them in your cooking repertoire.

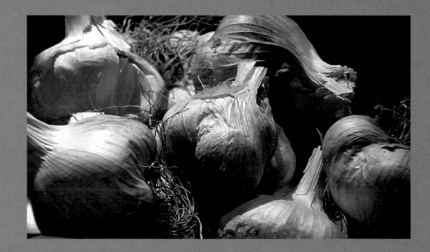

Alioli

Every European country on the Mediterranean claims credit for inventing this magnificent garlic mayonnaise. In Spain, and especially in Catalonia, the sauce is used to complement all sorts of meat, fish, vegetable, and rice dishes. The word comes from the Catalan words ali *(garlic) and* oli *(oil). Making this in a mortar may seem dangerously close to physical labor, but the smooth, creamy consistency of the garlic paste is difficult to achieve otherwise. The remainder can be done either with a whisk or a food processor. The sauce will keep in a tightly covered container in the refrigerator for up to 4 days.*

With a mortar and pestle, pound the garlic and salt together until it is a smooth, creamy paste.

In a food processor or using a whisk, process or beat together the egg yolks and water in a bowl until smooth. With the processor running or while continuously whisking, slowly pour in the oils, a few drops at first until the mixture emulsifies, and then in a slow, steady stream. You can add more water if the mixture becomes too thick. Add the vinegars and lemon juice. Mix in the garlic paste until smooth.

MAKES ABOUT 2 CUPS

2 cloves **garlic**

½ teaspoon **salt**

2 **egg yolks**

½ teaspoon **water**

¼ cup **extra virgin olive oil**

¾ cup **peanut oil**

½ teaspoon **red wine vinegar**

½ teaspoon **sherry vinegar**

Juice of 1 lemon

Romesco Sauce

MAKES ABOUT 2 CUPS

½ cup **hazelnuts**

½ cup **almonds**

4 **ñora chiles** (see page 87), stemmed and seeded

½ cup small hand-torn pieces **day-old baguette**

¾ cup **piquillo peppers** (see page 87)

1 clove **garlic**

¾ teaspoon **salt**

1 teaspoon **sugar**

1 tablespoon **Gallega Spice** (page 199)

¾ cup **olive oil**

1 tablespoon freshly squeezed **lemon juice**

1 teaspoon **sherry vinegar**

1 teaspoon **red wine vinegar**

This versatile sauce is a great accompaniment for all sorts of grilled or poached fish and seafood and for grilled vegetables, especially the marvelous spring onions (known colloquially as calçots*) so cherished in Catalonia. It's an easy sauce to make with a food processor and can be made a day ahead of time with one caution: don't fold in the roasted nuts until the day you are going to use it, or they will get soggy. If you can't get* ñora *chiles,* cascabels *are a good substitute, and any good roasted red pepper can replace the* piquillos. *The sauce will keep in a tightly covered container in the refrigerator for up to 4 days.*

Preheat the oven to 350°F. Roast the hazelnuts and almonds in separate sheet pans for about 10 minutes. Cut one of each nut open to check for doneness; the interiors should be a dark gold. When the nuts are cool enough to handle, remove the skins from the hazelnuts by rubbing them vigorously in a kitchen towel. Pulse the nuts in a food processor until they are a good mix of powder and coarse pieces. Remove and set aside.

Place the *ñora* chiles in a small saucepan with water to cover. Bring to a simmer, cook for 5 minutes, and then remove from the heat and let cool to room temperature in the liquid. When cool, remove the chiles and add the bread to absorb the chile water.

Combine the chiles, *piquillo* peppers, bread, garlic, salt, sugar, and spice mix in a food processor and process to a smooth paste. With the machine running, slowly add the oil, lemon juice, and vinegars, and process until well mixed. Pour into a bowl and fold in the nuts.

Mojo Sauces

These simple sauces are versions of classic accompaniments from the Canary Islands and are commonly eaten at room temperature with all sorts of fish, meat, and potatoes. Note that for the Mojo Picón, if you can't find ñora *chiles, substitute* cascabels.

Mojo Verde

Toss the cilantro leaves, garlic, and jalapeños in a medium bowl with ½ teaspoon of the salt and 2 tablespoons of the oil. Let stand for 20 minutes. Place the mixture in a food processor and process to a paste. With the machine running, add the remaining ¾ cup oil. Mix in the cumin and lime juice. Taste and adjust the seasoning.

Mojo Picón

Combine the chiles and vinegar in a small saucepan and bring to a boil. Immediately remove from the heat and allow the chiles to cool completely in the vinegar to soften.

With a mortar and pestle, pound the garlic and salt together to a smooth paste. In a food processor, combine the chiles and vinegar, the garlic paste, cumin, paprika, cayenne, thyme, oregano, and parsley, and process to a paste. With the machine running, slowly add the oil until the mixture emulsifies. Taste and adjust the seasoning.

Mojo Verde

MAKES ABOUT 1 CUP

2 bunches **cilantro**, stems removed

1 large clove **garlic**, coarsely chopped

2 **jalapeño chiles**, coarsely chopped

1½ teaspoons **salt**

2 tablespoons plus ¾ cup **extra virgin olive oil**

2 tablespoons **cumin seed**, toasted and ground (see page 199)

Juice of 1 lime

Mojo Picón

MAKES ABOUT 1 CUP

2 **ñora chile**s (see page 87), stemmed and seeded

1 **guajillo chile**, stemmed and seeded

¼ cup **red wine vinegar**

8 cloves **garlic**

¾ teaspoon **salt**

1 tablespoon **cumin seed**, toasted and ground (see page 199)

1 ½ teaspoons **paprika**

¼ teaspoon **cayenne pepper**

1½ teaspoons chopped fresh **thyme**

1½ teaspoons chopped fresh **oregano**

1 tablespoon chopped fresh **flat-leaf parsley**

½ cup **extra virgin olive oil**

Sofrito

MAKES ABOUT 1 CUP

¾ cup **extra virgin olive oil**

4 **yellow onions,** thinly sliced

4 cloves **garlic,** thinly sliced

4 cups diced **tomatoes**

1 teaspoon **saffron threads**

Sofrito *is not a dish unto itself, but is the all-important base for countless stews and other dishes in the Spanish repertoire, especially the huge array of rice dishes. It is the prime ingredient in our paella and* fideos. *Care must be taken to cook the* sofrito *slowly to meld all the flavors and reduce the mixture to a paste. You can make it well ahead of time and store it in the refrigerator until needed (it will keep for 3 to 4 weeks).*

Heat the oil over medium-high heat in a large, heavy-bottomed sauté pan. Add the onions, turn down the heat to low, and cook slowly until they are thoroughly caramelized, about 1 hour. The onions should have a dark caramel color and a soft texture and should taste sweet, almost like candy. Add the garlic and cook for another 15 minutes. Add the tomatoes and saffron and cook until the mixture has a thick, jamlike consistency, about 1 hour longer. Run through a food mill using the medium-holed plate or purée in a food processor until smooth.

Herb Oil

MAKES ABOUT 1 CUP

Several sprigs each **flat-leaf parsley, thyme, sage,** and **rosemary**

2 cloves **garlic,** crushed

1 cup **extra virgin olive oil**

Remove the herb leaves from their stems and chop finely. Mix the herbs, garlic, and oil together, and let stand for at least 1hour before using. Store in an airtight container for up to a week.

Spice Mixes

These easy-to-make spice blends can all be made in advance and stored in an airtight container in a cool, dark place (in other words, not on the stovetop) for months. However, to ensure peak freshness, it's best to make small batches that you will use up in a few weeks.

Cumin Spice

Toast the cumin in a small, dry pan over medium heat, stirring often, until lightly browned, about 5 minutes. Do the same with the coriander.

Using a spice grinder or a clean coffee grinder, grind the cumin, using an on-off pulse so that there is both powder and broken pieces. Transfer to a small bowl. Grind the coriander to a powder and add to the cumin. Add the remaining spices and mix well.

Gallega Spice

Combine all of the ingredients and store in a salt shaker.

Moruño Spice

Toast the cumin and coriander in a small, dry pan over medium heat, stirring often, until lightly browned, about 5 minutes. Using a spice grinder or clean coffee grinder, grind them both to a powder. Transfer to a small bowl, add the remaining spices, and mix well.

Cumin Spice

MAKES ABOUT 1 CUP

1 cup **cumin seed**

1 tablespoon **coriander seed**

1 tablespoon **paprika**

2 teaspoons **pimentón dulce** (see page 87)

1 teaspoon **cayenne pepper**

Gallega Spcie

MAKES ABOUT ¾ CUP

5 tablespoons **pimentón dulce** (see page 87)

3 tablespoons **pimentón picante** (see page 87)

3 tablespoons **paprika**

1 tablespoon **cayenne pepper**

Moruño Spice

MAKES ABOUT 1¼ CUPS

½ cup **cumin seed**

¼ cup **coriander seed**

1 tablespoon **black peppercorns**

1 tablespoon **paprika**

¼ cup **pimentón dulce** (see page 87)

2 teaspoons **cayenne pepper**

¼ cup **salt**

César Stocks

Making stocks from scratch is one of the easiest things to do, yet home cooks seldom take the time to do it. Stocks are among the basic building blocks for cooking in a restaurant kitchen, and they are one of the reasons that food in a restaurant often tastes richer, with deeper flavors, than meals prepared at home. One of the secrets to good meat stock lies in roasting the bones first. It brings out and concentrates the flavor, adding immeasurably to any dish in which the stock is used. The great thing about making stock is that the actual prep time is only a few minutes. The rest of the time involves roasting or simmering, leaving you free to do something else, like pour yourself a glass of wine and curl up with a good book as the aroma of the stock wafts through the house.

Shellfish Stock

Heat the oil over medium heat in a heavy-bottomed stockpot. Add the fennel, onion, carrots, celery, garlic, and jalapeño. Cover the pot and sweat the vegetables, stirring periodically, until they are a light caramel color, about 20 minutes. Stir in the shellfish and continue to cook until the shells are bright red, about 10 minutes. Add the tomato, wine, and brandy, and simmer for 3 minutes. Raise the heat to high, add the thyme, bay leaf, peppercorns, and water, and bring to a boil. Turn the heat down to a simmer and cook, uncovered, for 45 minutes, periodically skimming off the foam that rises to the top. Strain through a fine sieve. Let cool, cover, and refrigerate for up to 2 days or freeze for up to 1 month.

Shellfish Stock

MAKES ABOUT 6 CUPS

¼ cup **extra virgin olive oil**

1 small bulb **fennel**, coarsely chopped

1 medium **yellow onion**, coarsely chopped

2 large **carrots**, peeled and coarsely chopped

2 **celery** stalks, coarsely chopped

1 head **garlic**, cut in half crosswise

1 **jalapeño chile**, coarsely chopped

5 pounds **lobster**, **shrimp**, or **crab**, coarsely chopped, or an equivalent weight in shells

1 fresh or canned **tomato**, coarsely chopped

½ cup **dry white wine**

¼ cup **brandy**

6 sprigs **thyme**

1 **bay leaf**

5 **black peppercorns**

8 cups cold **water**

Roasted Chicken or Pork Stock

Chicken or Pork Stock

MAKES ABOUT 8 CUPS

5 pounds **chicken bones** or **pork bones** (preferably pork necks)

¼ cup **extra virgin olive oil**

1 small bulb **fennel**, coarsely chopped

1 **yellow onion**, coarsely chopped

2 large **carrots**, peeled and coarsely chopped

2 **celery** stalks, coarsely chopped

1 head **garlic**, cut in half crosswise

1 **jalapeño chile**, coarsely chopped

6 sprigs **thyme**

1 **bay leaf**

5 **black peppercorns**

12 cups cold **water**

1 can (6 ounces) **tomato paste**

Our recipes for chicken and pork stock are identical, save for the type of bones called for, so we have combined them.

Preheat the oven to 450°F. Spread the chicken or pork pieces on a sheet pan in a single layer so they will brown evenly. Roast until nicely browned, about 30 minutes.

Heat the oil over medium heat in a heavy-bottomed stockpot. Add the fennel, onion, carrots, celery, garlic, and jalapeño. Cover the pot and sweat the vegetables, stirring periodically, until they are a light caramel color, about 20 minutes. Add the roasted bones, thyme, bay leaf, peppercorns, water, and tomato paste, raise the heat to high, and bring to a boil. Turn the heat down to a low simmer and cook, uncovered, for 6 hours, periodically skimming off the foam that rises to the top. Strain the stock through a fine sieve. Let cool, cover, and refrigerate until well chilled, then lift off and discard the fat.

Fried Croutons

Fried Croutons

1 day-old **baguette**

2 cups **olive oil**

Salt and freshly ground **black pepper**

These are a great accompaniment to all sorts of soups, but they are particularly good with our Gazpacho (page 92) and English Cucumber Gazpacho (page 94). The sliced croutons go with our Portuguese-Style Fish Stew (page 155). The croutons be made several days ahead of time and stored in an airtight container.

Cut away the crust on the baguette, and tear the bread into ½-inch, irregularly shaped pieces; or cut into ¼-inch slices, leaving the crust on. In a deep, heavy-bottomed pan, heat the oil to 375°F. Fry the bread in small batches until a light golden brown. Remove the croutons with a slotted spoon and drain on paper towels, then toss them in a large bowl with salt and pepper to taste. If not using immediately, cool and store in an airtight container.

Cleaning Squid

Cut off the tentacles just above the eye. Pinch the cut end of the tentacles and squeeze out the beak, which looks like a small bean. Discard the beak and reserve the tentacles.

Hold the uncut end of the squid body with your fingers, and scrape the length of the body with the back of a knife to squeeze out the entrails. Discard the entrails and leave the skin on.

A small quill-like appendage will be sticking out of the body. Stick the point of a knife into the quill and pull the body away. Discard the quill. Rinse the body well inside and out.

The body is now ready for stuffing, or you can cut it into rings.

Resources

Most of the ingredients called for in the tapas recipes can be obtained from your local supermarket. However, some of the Spanish specialty products may be more difficult to find. The following resources all offer mail order.

La Española
25020 Doble Avenue
Harbor City, CA 90710
310-539-0455
www.laespanolameats.com
www.donajuana.com

Located in southern California, this company specializes in the meats and cheeses of Spain, and all their products are flown in direct. An excellent source for chorizo, jamón, *and cheeses.*

The Spanish Table
1427 Western Avenue
Seattle, WA 98101
206-682-2827

1814 San Pablo Avenue
Berkeley, CA 94702
510-548-1383

109 Guadalupe Street
Santa Fe, NM 87501
505-986-0243
www.tablespan.com

Owner Steve Winston has what is probably the only retail store in the country devoted to the food products of the Iberian peninsula, including a vast selection of Spanish wines, sherries, and port, as well as books, music, tableware, and churro *presses. If you are lucky enough to live in either Seattle (the original shop), Berkeley, or Santa Fe, drop in. Otherwise, you can purchase anything by phone or online.*

Stephen Singer Olio
SsingerOlio@earthlink.net
510-845-0693

Stephen is one of the partners in César, and he also imports a line of high-quality Italian olive oils and vinegars.

Tienda.com
888-472-1022
757-220-1143
Fax 757-564-0779
www.tienda.com
contact@tienda.com

This relatively small, family-run company carries a full range of Spanish products, including hams, chorizo, and an assortment of canned seafood. From April to September they sell pimientos de Padrón.

Zingerman's Delicatessen
888-638-8162
Fax 734-477-6988
www.zingermans.com

While not strictly Spanish, this is one of the best specialty food stores in the country. It carries a staggering selection of olive oils, vinegars, chiles, and many of the other products we use. It also stocks a vast assortment of cheeses, meats, and baked goods.

∽∽

César
1515 Shattuck Avenue
Berkeley, CA 94708
510-883-0222
info@barcesar.com
www.barcesar.com

Our own website offers information about our food and drink, César special events, and links to related sites.

Authors' Information
www.whoisitanyway.com

The authors' website has links to resources and information.

Bibliography

Food and Tapas

Aidells, Bruce, and Denis Kelly. *Hot Links and Country Flavors.* New York: Knopf, 1990.

Aris, Pepita. *The Spanish Woman's Kitchen.* New York: Sterling Publishing, 1992.

Casas, Penelope. *Delicioso!* New York: Knopf, 1996.

———. *The Foods & Wines of Spain.* New York: Knopf, 1979.

———. *Paella.* New York: Knopf, 1999.

———. *Tapas.* New York: Knopf, 1985.

Domingo, Xavier, and Pierre Hussenot. *The Taste of Spain.* Paris: Flammarion, 1992.

English, Todd, and Sally Sampson. *The Olives Table.* New York: Simon & Schuster, 1997.

Torrez, Marimar. *The Catalan Country Kitchen.* Berkeley: Aris Books, 1992.

———. *The Spanish Table.* New York: Doubleday, 1986.

Tropp, Barbara. *The China Moon Cookbook.* New York: Workman Publishing, 1992.

Trutter, Marion, ed. *Culinaria: Spain.* Cologne: Könemann, 1998.

Wolfert, Paula. *Couscous & Other Good Food of Morocco.* New York: Harper & Row, 1973.

Cocktails and Spirits

Calabrese, Salvatore. *Classic Cocktails.* New York: Sterling Publishing, 1997.

Collins, Philip. *The Art of the Cocktail.* San Francisco: Chronicle Books, 1992.

Conrad III, Barnaby. *The Martini.* San Francisco: Chronicle Books, 1995.

Gabányi, Stefan. *Whisk(e)y.* New York: Abbeville Press, 1997.

Pacult, F. Paul. *Kindred Spirits.* New York: Hyperion, 1997.

Regan, Gary. *The Bartender's Bible.* New York: Harper Collins Publishers, 1991.

Schumann, Charles. *American Bar.* New York: Abbeville Press, 1995.

———. *Tropical Bar Book.* New York: Stewart, Tabori & Chang, 1989.

Spalding, Jill. *Blithe Spirits.* Washington, D.C.: Rosenbaum/Acropolis Books, 1988.

Waggoner, Susan, and Robert Markel. *Vintage Cocktails.* New York: Stewart, Tabori & Chang, 1999.

Index